Be prepared...
To learn...
To succeed...

Get **REA**dy. It all starts here. REA's preparation for the Florida Algebra I EOC is fully aligned with the Next Generation Sunshine State Standards.

Free!
2 Practice Tests Online

www.rea.com

Visit us online at *www.rea.com*

Ready, Set, Go!®

FLORIDA
End-of-Course Assessment
Algebra 1

Elizabeth Morrison, Ed.D.
Valencia Community College, West Campus
Orlando, Florida

Jodie Carleton, B.S.
Strawberry Crest High School
Plant, Florida

Research & Education Association

The benchmarks presented in this book were created and implemented
by the Florida Department of Education (FLDOE).
For further information, visit the FLDOE website at *http://fcat.fldoe.org.*

Research & Education Association
61 Ethel Road West
Piscataway, New Jersey 08854
E-mail: info@rea.com

Ready, Set, Go!®
Florida Algebra 1: End-of-Course Assessment

Printed in the United States of America

Library of Congress Control Number 2011942951

ISBN-13: 978-0-7386-1022-1
ISBN-10: 0-7386-1022-4

REA® *Ready, Set, Go!*® are registered trademarks of
Research & Education Association, Inc.

Contents

Two additional online practice tests at www.rea.com

About Research & Education Association

Founded in 1959, Research & Education Association (REA) is dedicated to publishing the finest and most effective educational materials—including software, study guides, and test preps—for students in elementary school, middle school, high school, college, graduate school, and beyond.

Today, REA's wide-ranging catalog is a leading resource for teachers, students, and professionals.

Acknowledgments

In addition to our authors, we would like to thank Larry B. Kling, Vice President, Editorial, for his overall guidance, which brought this publication to completion; Pam Weston, Publisher, for setting the quality standards for production integrity and managing the publication to completion; Alice Leonard, Senior Editor, for project management; Mel Friedman, Lead Math Editor, for his technical review of the math content; and Fred Grayson of American BookWorks Corporation for overseeing manuscript development and typesetting.

We also extend our gratitude to Robert Bashear, mathematics department head, Sickles High School, Tampa, Florida; James Fusco of Tampa Bay Technical High School, Tampa, Florida; and Joan Rosebush, professor of mathematics, University of Vermont.

About Our Authors

Elizabeth Morrison is a mathematics instructor at Valencia College in Orlando, Florida, and has taught developmental and college-level mathematics for over 30 years. She received her bachelor's and master's degrees in mathematics from Florida State University and her doctorate of education in Curriculum and Instruction from the University of Central Florida. At Valencia College, Elizabeth has worked extensively in the area of professional development with new faculty as they complete the process to secure tenure.

Jodie Carleton is a high school teacher of mathematics at Strawberry Crest High School, Plant, Florida. She teaches Algebra I ICL ("I Can Learn" system).

Introduction

Passing the Florida Algebra 1 EOC Test

About This Book

This book, along with REA's true-to-format online practice tests, provides you with the most up-to-date information about the Florida Algebra 1 End-of-Course Assessment. Known simply as the Algebra 1 EOC, this computer-based test measures your mastery of first-year Algebra.

Here you'll find everything you need to know about the test combined with all the practice you need to prepare for test day. Because one of the proven strategies to achieving better performance on any standardized test is practice, we give you four full-length practice tests (two in the book and two online at *www.rea.com*, complete with detailed explanations. Each of our eight review chapters covers one of the major Algebra 1 subject areas and shows you how each area will be tested. We use a step-by-step approach to help you build your knowledge and confidence, with full explanations and extensive examples.

About the Test

The Florida EOC Assessments are part of Florida's Next Generation Strategic Plan, which is designed to increase student achievement and improve college and career readiness. EOC assessments are computer-based, criterion-referenced assessments that measure specific standards that have been developed for several courses, including Algebra 1, Biology 1, Geometry, and U.S. History.

How is this test given?

For the majority of students, the EOC assessments are computer-based. Exceptions are made for students with disabilities who need to take EOC assessments on paper.

Format of the Test

The Algebra 1 EOC assessment includes two types of test items: approximately 35-40 multiple-choice items (MC) and 25-30 fill-in response items (FR). You will also have a reference sheet that you can consult. According to the state's specifications, multiple-choice questions should take an average of one minute to answer. You should allocate about $1\frac{1}{2}$ minutes per fill-in question. You will be allowed to use a calculator on this exam.

Who takes this test?

All students enrolled in and completing the following courses take the Algebra 1 EOC:

- Algebra 1

- Algebra 1 Honors

- Algebra 1B

- Pre-AICE Mathematics 1

- IB Middle Years Program – Algebra 1 Honors

Computerized Testing

Practice Tests

Prior to taking the Algebra 1 EOC Assessment, students are required to participate in a practice-test session at their school in order to become familiar with the testing tools and platform. These are computer-based practice tests, called Electronic Practice Assessment Tools (ePATs). The online computerized practice tests included with this book will give students a valuable head start.

E-Tools for Exam Day

The tools and resources available to you on test day will vary slightly depending on the subject area assessed. All students taking a computer-based assessment will have access to the following e-tools in the computer-based platform:

- **Review**: Students use this e-tool to mark questions to be reviewed at a later time. Before exiting the assessment and submitting their responses, students are taken to a screen that identifies questions that are answered, unanswered, and marked for review.

- **Eliminate Choice**: Students use this tool to mark answer choices that they wish to eliminate.

- **Highlighter**: Students use this tool to highlight sections of the question or passage.

- **Eraser**: Students use the eraser to remove marks made by the highlighter or the eliminate-choice tool.

- **Help**: Students may click the Help icon to learn more about the e-tools. The Help text appears in a separate window.

- **Calculator**: Students are provided access to a calculator, which appears in a pop-up window. For Algebra 1, students use a four-function calculator.

- **Straightedge**: Students are provided a straightedge e-tool, which looks like a ruler without measuring units. Students use the straightedge as they would use the edge of a piece of paper to help work a problem.

- **Exhibit**: Students are provided a reference sheet of commonly used formulas and conversions to work the test questions. The reference sheet appears in a pop-up window under the exhibit icon.

Students are also provided directions for completing fill-in response questions and a diagram and helpful hints for the appropriate calculator under the exhibit icon.

In addition to the e-tools, students are also provided work folders to use as scratch paper to work out the problems. Schools may also permit students to use approved hand-held calculators, and can also provide paper versions of the reference sheet.

Overview of the Algebra 1 EOC Assessment

This test is aligned with Florida's Next Generation Sunshine State Standards. These standards are presented below.

Standards

Algebra	
Standard 1	Real and Complex Number System
Standard 2	Relations and Functions
Standard 3	Linear Equations and Inequalities
Standard 4	Polynomials
Standard 5	Rational Expressions and Equations
Standard 6	Radical Expressions and Equations
Standard 7	Quadratic Equations
Standard 10	Mathematical Reasoning and Problem Solving
Discrete Mathematics	
Standard 7	Set Theory
Geometry	
Standard 1	Points, Lines, Angles, and Planes

Benchmarks

The following are the specific standards and benchmarks of the Algebra 1 EOC Assessment.

Strand A: Algebra

MA.912.A.1.8   Use the zero product property of real numbers in a variety of contexts to identify solutions to equations.

MA.912.A.2.3   Describe the concept of a function, use function notation, determine whether a given relation is a function, and link equations to functions.

MA.912.A.2.4   Determine the domain and range of a relation.

MA.912.A.2.13   Solve real-world problems involving relations and functions.

MA.912.A.3.1   Solve linear equations in one variable that include simplifying algebraic expressions.

MA.912.A.3.2   Identify and apply the distributive, associative, and commutative properties of real numbers and the properties of equality.

MA.912.A.3.3   Solve literal equations for a specified variable.

MA.912.A.3.4   Solve and graph simple and compound inequalities in one variable and be able to justify each step in a solution.

MA.912.A.3.5   Symbolically represent and solve multi-step and real-world applications that involve linear equations and inequalities.

MA.912.A.3.7   Rewrite equations of a line into slope-intercept form and standard form.

MA.912.A.3.8   Graph a line given any of the following information: a table of values, the x-and y-intercepts, two points, the slope and a point, the equation of the line in slope-intercept form, standard form, or point-slope form.

MA.912.A.3.9   Determine the slope, x-intercept, and y-intercept of a line given its graph, its equation, or two points on the line.

MA.912.A.3.10   Write an equation of a line given any of the following information: two points on the line, its slope and one point on the line, or its graph. Also, find an equation of a new line parallel to a given line, or perpendicular to a given line, through a given point on the new line.

MA.912.A.3.11 Write an equation of a line that models a data set and use the equation or the graph to make predictions. Describe the slope of the line in terms of the data, recognizing that the slope is the rate of change.

MA.912.A.3.12 Graph a linear equation or inequality in two variables with and without graphing technology. Write an equation or inequality represented by a given graph.

MA.912.A.3.13 Use a graph to approximate the solution of a system of linear equations or inequalities in two variables with and without technology.

MA.912.A.3.14 Solve systems of linear equations and inequalities in two and three variables using graphical, substitution, and elimination methods.

MA.912.A.3.15 Solve real-world problems involving systems of linear equations and inequalities in two and three variables.

MA.912.A.4.1 Simplify monomials and monomial expressions using the laws of integral exponents.

MA.912.A.4.2 Add, subtract, and multiply polynomials.

MA.912.A.4.3 Factor polynomial expressions.

MA.912.A.4.4 Divide polynomials by monomials and polynomials with various techniques, including synthetic division.

MA.912.A.5.1 Simplify algebraic ratios.

MA.912.A.5.4 Solve algebraic proportions.

MA.912.A.6.1 Simplify radical expressions.

MA.912.A.6.2 Add, subtract, multiply, and divide radical expressions (square roots and higher).

MA.912.A.7.1 Graph quadratic equations with and without graphing technology.

MA.912.A.7.2 Solve quadratic equations over the real numbers by factoring and by using the quadratic formula.

MA.912.A.7.8 Use quadratic equations to solve real-world problems.

MA.912.A.10.1 Use a variety of problem-solving strategies, such as drawing a diagram, making a chart, guessing and checking, solving a simpler problem, writing an equation, working backwards, and creating a table.

MA.912.A.10.2 Decide whether a solution is reasonable in the context of the original situation.

Strand B: Discrete Mathematics

MA.912.D.7.1 Perform set operations such as union and intersection, complement, and cross product.

MA.912.D.7.2 Use Venn diagrams to explore relationships and patterns and to make arguments about relationships between sets.

Strand C: Geometry

MA.912.G.1.4 Use coordinate geometry to find slopes, parallel lines, perpendicular lines, and equations of lines.

What to Do before the Test

- **Pay attention in class.**

- **Carefully work through the chapters and problems in this book.** Mark any topics that you find difficult and rework them.

- **Take the practice tests and become familiar with the format of the Algebra 1 EOC Assessment.** Try to take these tests under simulated conditions—time yourself, stay calm, and pace yourself. As we said earlier, multiple-choice questions should take about one minute and the fill-in questions about $1\frac{1}{2}$ minutes. We make this easy with our online practice tests, which provide a timed, auto-scored experience. (*www.rea.co*m)

What to Do During the Test

- **Read the questions carefully to make sure you understand what is being asked of you.** Every word in the question gets you that much closer to the answer.

- **Read all of the possible answers.** Even if you think you have found the correct response, do not automatically assume that it is the best answer. Read through each answer choice to be sure you are not jumping to conclusions.

- **Use the process of elimination in multiple-choice questions.** This is one of the best techniques in solving these types of questions. Try to eliminate those choices that appear obviously incorrect. For each one you can eliminate, you've increased your odds dramatically of answering correctly. If you eliminate two choices, for example, you now have a 50% chance of answering the question correctly.

- **Work on the easier questions first.** If you find yourself working too long on one question, move on to the next question. When you've reached the end of the test, there will be a window on the computer that will pop up and tell you which questions were unanswered so you can go back to them.

- **Be aware of the correct units.** If the question asks for *meters*, make sure you're not selecting an answer choice that looks correct, but is in *feet*.

- **In fill-in response questions, make sure your answer is complete.** Again, check the types of units of measurement. For example, is the test asking for square inches or cubic inches?

- **Answer all of the questions.** You will not be penalized for incorrect answers, so you'll increase your chances of improving your score by guessing. Even one "good guess" can increase your score by a point.

- *Relax.*

Good luck!

Chapter 1

Linear Equations and Inequalities

This section develops the following skills:

1. You should be able to solve equations using inverse operations.

2. You should be able to understand the effects of solving the equations using the Order of Operations.

3. You will need to determine how many steps it takes to solve each problem and be able to explain the process. This is especially true for "Real World" problems.

Standards

The following standards are assessed on the Florida's Algebra 1 End-of-Course Assessment either directly or indirectly:

MA.912.A.3.1* (Moderate) Solve linear equations in one variable that include simplifying algebraic expressions.

MA.912.A.3.2** Identify and apply the distributive, associative, and commutative properties of real numbers and the properties of equality.

MA.912.A.3.3* (Moderate) Solve literal equations for a specified variable.

MA.912.A.3.5* (Moderate) Symbolically represents and solves multi-step and real-world applications that involve linear equations and inequalities.

MA.912.A.3.6 (Moderate) (Honors only) Solve and graph the solutions of absolute value equations and inequalities with one variable.

MA.912.A.5.4* (Low) Solve algebraic proportions.

MA.912.A.10.1** Use a variety of problem-solving strategies, such as drawing a diagram, making a chart, guess-and-check, solving a simpler problem, writing an equation, working backwards, and creating a table.

MA.912.A.10.2** (Moderate): Decide whether a solution is reasonable in the context of the original situation.

MA.912.A.10.3** Decide whether a given statement is always, sometimes, or never true (statements involving linear or quadratic expressions, equations, or inequalities rational or radical expressions or logarithmic or exponential functions).

LA.910.3.1.3** The student will prewrite by using organizational strategies and tools (e.g., technology, spreadsheet, outline, chart, table, graph, Venn Diagram, web, story map, plot pyramid) to develop a personal organizational style.

These standards will be tested with a variety of questions that are characterized as of **low**, **moderate**, and **high** difficulty. Difficulty is different from complexity. Just because a problem has several steps does not mean that its difficulty level is high. All of the steps of a particular problem could be considered of "low" difficulty, which means that the problem is complex and time consuming, but not necessarily difficult. Difficulty is determined by how much thinking or background knowledge is involved in solving the problem.

So what do you actually need to know? You need to understand Order of Operations and the inverse operations. You also need to be able to solve 1-step, 2-step, and multi-step equations, as well as literal equations.

Order of operations

What is "Order of Operations"?

First − Parentheses

Second − Exponents

Third — Multiplication or division, whichever comes first, from left to right

Fourth — Addition or subtraction, whichever comes first, from left to right.

Many times the "Order of Operations" is referred to as **PEMDAS.** You may also remember the "Order of Operations" as **P**lease **E**xcuse **M**y **D**ear **A**unt **S**ally. So read the problem from left to right just like you would read a book. Look for any set of parentheses and perform the operation inside the parentheses first, then look for "exponents" and take their number or variable to the power of the exponent. Then perform any multiplication or division from left to right in the problem. Finally, you must perform any addition or subtraction from left to right that you see in the problem.

Example:

$$(4+3) - 2^2 + 8/4 + 12 - 10 = ?$$

Solve what is inside the **parentheses** first: $(4 + 3) = 7$

Now the problem says $7 - 2^2 + 8/4 + 12 - 10$

Next we will take care of the **exponent** so: $-2^2 = -4$. It is important to note that $(-2)^2$ is entirely different than -2^2. When you see -2^2, the negative sign in front of the 2 stays the same and you get -4, while $(-2)^2$ means that a negative number is being squared and the result of this "squaring" will be a $+4$.

$$7 - 4 + 8/4 + 12 - 10 =$$
$$7 - 4 + 2 + 12 - 10 =$$
$$3 + 2 + 12 - 10 =$$
$$5 + 12 - 10 =$$
$$17 - 10 =$$
$$7$$

Example:

$$\frac{3-2^2+(5-8)}{2}$$

Remember to follow your order of operations!

$$\frac{3-2^2-3}{2}$$ Simplify the parentheses and then work in the exponent.

$$\frac{3-4-3}{2}$$ Simplify the top and then divide by 2.

$$\frac{-4}{2}=-2$$

Example:

$$\frac{12}{6}+3^3-28$$ exponents first

$$\frac{12}{6}+27-28$$ divide

$$2 + 27 - 28$$ add

$$29 - 28 = 1$$

One-step equations

One-step equations require exactly one step to solve for the variable (letter used in the equation).

For example: $x + 2 = 11$

Step 1: Undo the addition or subtraction with the inverse (opposite) operation. The inverse will be used on both sides of the equation for balance. The golden rule is, Whatever you do to one side of the equation, you must do the exact same action to the other side of the equation.

Step 1   Undo the addition of 2 by subtracting 2. Subtracting 2 is the opposite operation of adding 2.

$$x + 2 = 11$$
$$\underline{-2 = -2}$$
$$x \quad\;\; = 9$$

If the 2 in the original equation was subtracted from x, then you use addition to isolate x.

Example:

$$5 + x = 3$$

$$5 + x = 3$$
$$\underline{-5 \quad\;\; -5}$$
$$x = -2$$

Subtract 5 from both sides.

Example:

$$2x = 6$$

$$\frac{2x}{2} = \frac{6}{2}$$
$$x = 3$$

Divide both sides by 2

Example:

$$9x = -27$$

$$\frac{9x}{9} = \frac{-27}{9}$$
$$x = -3$$

Divide both sides by 9

Example:

$\dfrac{x}{5} = 10$ Multiply both sides by 5

$(5)\dfrac{x}{5} = 10(5)$ 5's cancel out on the left hand side

$x = 50$

Two-step equations

Example of a two-step equation: $3x + 2 = 11$

Note that this two-step equation is similar to the equation above, but a 3 was placed in front of the variable. The 3 means that you are actually multiplying the 3 and x together. So, you'll need to solve this problem by using inverse operations. In other words, perform the order of operations in reverse.

Step 1   Just like before the student will use the inverse operation of subtraction to "undo" the addition of 2. You now have

$$\begin{array}{r} 3x + 2 = 11 \\ -2 = -2 \\ \hline 3x \quad\;\; = 9 \end{array}$$

Step 2   Since the variable, x, is being multiplied by the 3, the inverse operation would be to divide both sides by 3.

$$\dfrac{3x}{3} = \dfrac{9}{3}$$
$$x = 3$$

The answer for x is 3.

Example:

$5x + 2 = 27$ Subtract 2 from both sides

$\quad\; -2 = -2$

$\dfrac{5x}{5} = \dfrac{25}{5}$ Divide both sides by 5

$x = 5$

Example:

$$3x - 3 = 15$$

$$\begin{array}{r} 3x - 3 = 15 \\ \underline{+3 \ + 3} \\ 3x \quad\ = 18 \end{array}$$ Add 3 to both sides

$$\frac{3x}{3} = \frac{18}{3}$$ Divide both sides by 3

$$x = 6$$

Multi-step equations

The multi-step equation is a continuation of the "walking process." The multi-step equation needs multiple steps to be solved. This type of equation usually involves having variables on both sides of the equal sign.

For instance: $3x + 5 = 5x - 1$

For this problem, the student will need to move the -1 to the other side of the equal sign by using the opposite operation, that is, by adding 1 to both sides of the equation.

$$\begin{array}{r} 3x + 5 = 5x - 1 \\ \underline{+ 1 = \quad\ + 1} \\ 3x + 6 = 5x \end{array}$$

Now we have

You will need to move the $3x$ to the other side of the equal sign. Variables are moved just like constants by using inverse operations. Since $3x$ is added, we subtract it from each side.

So subtract $3x$ $$\begin{array}{r} 3x + 6 = 5x \\ \underline{-3x \quad\ = -3x} \\ 6 = 2x \end{array}$$ (from above)

Since $2x$ is multiplication you will to divide both sides of the equation by 2. $$\frac{6}{2} = \frac{2x}{2}$$

$x = 3$ is the final answer.

Here is another type of a **multi-step equation**:

$$2(3x + 5) = 2x - 2$$

With this type of problem, you must "clean up" the problem first. In other words, you will need to take care of the $(3x + 5)$ that is being multiplied by the 2.

Distributive property

First, you will need to use the **distributive property**. The **distributive property** states that for any numbers a, b, and c, $a(b+c) = ab+ac$. This means that b is multiplied by a, the c is multiplied by a and the result of ab is added to the result of ac. Let's look at some examples of the distributive property using numbers instead of letters.

Example:
$$\begin{aligned} 2(3+5) &= 2(3) + 2(5) \\ &= 6 + 10 \\ &= 16 \end{aligned} \quad \text{or} \quad \begin{aligned} 2(9-3) &= 2(9) - 2(3) \\ &= 18 - 6 \\ &= 12 \end{aligned}$$

So let's look back at the previous problem that has the distributive property and variables.

$$2(3x+5) = 2x - 2$$

First use the distributive property
$$2(3x) + 2(5) = 2x - 2$$

Now we have
$$6x + 10 = 2x - 2$$

The $+10$ will need to move to the other side of the equation by using the inverse operation of subtracting -10.
$$\begin{aligned} 6x + 10 &= 2x - 2 \\ -10 &= \quad -10 \end{aligned}$$

The result is
$$6x = 2x - 12$$

The next step is to move the positive $2x$ to the other side of the equal sign by using the inverse operation of subtracting $2x$.
$$\begin{aligned} 6x &= 2x - 12 \\ -2x &= -2x \end{aligned}$$

The answer so far is $\qquad$ $4x = -12$

"Undo" the multiplication of 4 and x by dividing both sides of the equation by 4.

$$\frac{4x}{4} = \frac{-12}{4}$$

Your final answer is $\qquad$ $x = -3.$

Literal Equations

A literal equation contains more than one variable in the equation. When solving you will not get an answer like =5, instead we are just going to rearrange the variables.

Example:

Solve for l

$A = lw$

Since we are solving for l move all other number and variable to the other side of the equation. Make sure we move w and not l.

$A = lw$ $\qquad$ Divide both sides by w

$$\frac{A}{w} = \frac{lw}{w}$$

Thus $\dfrac{A}{w} = l$ or $l = \dfrac{A}{w}$

Example:

Solve for t

$w = tmz$ $\qquad$ Divide both sides by mz

$$\frac{w}{mz} = \frac{twz}{mz}$$

Thus $\dfrac{w}{mz} = t$ or $t = \dfrac{w}{mz}$

Example:

Solve for b

$abc = f + e$ Divide both sides by ac.

$$\frac{abc}{ac} = \frac{f+e}{ac}$$

$$b = \frac{f+e}{ac}$$

Example:

Solve for x

$\dfrac{xy}{z} = v$ Multiply both sides by z.

$$(z)\frac{xy}{z} = v(z)$$

$xy = vz$ Divide both sides by y.

$$\frac{xy}{y} = \frac{vz}{y}$$

$$x = \frac{vz}{y}$$

Inequalities

$<$ less than
$>$ greater than
$\leq$ less than or equal to
$\geq$ greater than or equal to

Solving for inequalities involving a variable is just like solving a normal equation.

Let's try some examples.

Example:

$x - 2 \geq 5$

$$
\begin{array}{l}
x - 2 \geq 5 \\
\underline{+2 \ + \ 2} \\
x \quad\ \geq 7
\end{array}
$$

Add 2 to both sides.

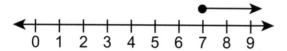

Example:

$3x < 9$ Divide both sides by 3.

$\dfrac{3x}{3} < \dfrac{9}{3}$

$x < 3$

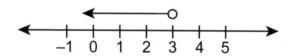

Example:

$\dfrac{x}{5} > 25$

$(5)\dfrac{x}{5} > 25(5)$ Multiply both sides by 5.

$x > 125$

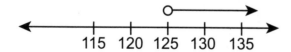

Example:

$$-2x + 5 \leq 23$$
$$\underline{\quad -5 \quad -5 \quad}$$ Subtract 5 from both sides.
$$-2x \qquad \leq 18$$

$$\frac{-2x}{-2} \geq \frac{18}{-2}$$ Divide both sides by -2 and reverse the sign.

$$x \geq -9$$

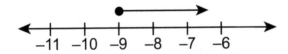

Example:

$$2(-3x + 1) \geq 14$$ Distribute.

$$-6x + 2 \geq 14$$
$$\underline{\quad -2 \quad -2 \quad}$$ Subtract 2 from both sides. Then divide both sides by -6
$$-6x \quad \geq \quad 12$$ and reverse the sign.

$$\frac{-6x}{-6} \leq \frac{12}{-6}$$

$$x \leq -2$$

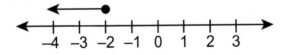

Absolute Value

Absolute value is the distance a number is from zero on a number line.

$|5|$ is read as the "absolute value of 5."

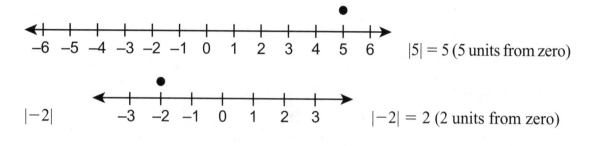

$|5| = 5$ (5 units from zero)

$|-2|$ $|-2| = 2$ (2 units from zero)

Now let's solve some problems involving absolute value.

$|-4| + |3| =$

Rewrite the problem applying the absolute value rules.

$4 + 3 = 7$

A. $|x + 3| = 9$

Remember absolute value is a distance from zero. Since we have two distances from zero, we will have two equations to solve.

| 1. Isolate absolute value bars. |
| 2. Write two equations. |
| 3. Solve each |
| 4. Check answers and plug into original. |

$x + 3 = 9$ $x + 3 = -(9)$ [reverse sign]
$x = 6$ $x = -12$

$|(6) + 3| = 9$ $|(-12) + 3| = 9$
$|9| = 9$ ✓ $|-9)| = 9$ ✓

The solutions, therefore, are $x = 6$ and $x = -12$

B. $|2x - 5| - 3 = 8$
                $+3 \quad +3$

$$|2x - 5| = 11$$

$$
\begin{array}{ll}
2x - 5 = 11 & 2x - 5 = -(11) \\
2x = 16 & 2x = -6 \\
x = 8 & x = -3
\end{array}
$$

Check your solutions.

$$
\begin{array}{ll}
|2(8) - 5| - 3 = 8 & |2(-3) - 5| - 3 = 8 \\
|11| - 3 = 8 & |-11| - 3 = 8 \\
8 = 8 \checkmark & 8 = 8 \checkmark
\end{array}
$$

C. $|x + 5| - 2 = -5$

$$|x + 5| = -3$$

$$
\begin{array}{ll}
x + 5 = -3 & x + 5 = -(-3) \\
x = -8 & x + 5 = 3 \\
 & x = 2
\end{array}
$$

Check your solutions.

$$
\begin{array}{ll}
|-8 + 5| = -3 & |(-2) + 5| = -3 \\
|-3| = -3 \ \times & |3| = -3 \ \times
\end{array}
$$

No solution!

D. $|6x + 4| = 8x + 10$

$$
\begin{array}{ll}
6x + 4 = 8x + 10 & 6x + 4 = -(8x + 10) \\
4 = 2x + 10 & 6x + 4 = -8x - 10 \\
-6 = 2x & 4 = -14x - 10 \\
-3 = x & 14 = -14x \\
 & -1 = x
\end{array}
$$

Check your solutions.

$|6(-3) + 4| = 8(-3) + 10$ $|6(-1) + 4| = 8(-1) + 10$

$|-18 + 4| = -24 - 10$ $|-6 + 4| = -8 + 10$

$|-14| = -14$ $|-2| = 2$

$14 = -14$ ✗ $2 = 2$ ✓

$$x = -1$$

Absolute Value Inequalities

We use the same process as an absolute value equations ($=$) but we will have an inequality symbol ($>, <, \geq, \leq$) instead.

TIPS:

- We will still have two problems to solve.

- $>, \geq$ think of "great**or**" becoming an "OR" inequality.

- $<, \leq$ think less th**an** becoming an "AND" inequality.

A. $|3x - 1| > 5$

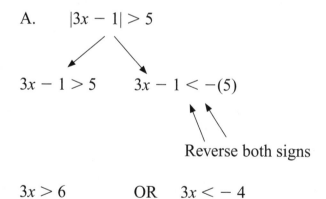

$3x - 1 > 5$ $3x - 1 < -(5)$

Reverse both signs

$3x > 6$ OR $3x < -4$

$x > 2$ OR $x < -\dfrac{4}{3}$

1. Isolate Absolute values
2. Write two inequalities
3. Decide if AND/OR inequality
4. Graph:
   or
   and

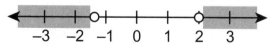

Any number in the shaded region makes *at least one* inequality true.

B. $|6x - 8| + 3 \leq 27$

$$|6x - 8| \leq 24$$

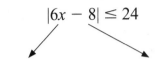

$6x - 8 \leq 24$ $6x - 8 \geq -24$

$6x \leq 32$ AND $6x \geq -16$

$x \leq \dfrac{32}{6}$ $x \geq \dfrac{-16}{6}$ or $\dfrac{-8}{3}$

$x \leq \dfrac{16}{3}$ or $5\dfrac{1}{3}$

$-\dfrac{8}{3} \leq x \leq \dfrac{16}{3}$ $x \geq \dfrac{-8}{3}$ and $x \leq \dfrac{16}{3}$

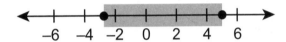

Any number in the shaded region makes *both* inequalities true.

C. $|4x + 2| \geq -18$

$4x + 2 \geq -18$ $4x + 2 \leq 18$

$4x \geq -20$ $4x \leq 16$

$x \geq -5$ OR $x \leq 4$

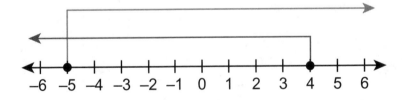

The solution is all real numbers.

End-of-Chapter Quiz: Linear Equations and Inequalities

1. Solve $4(3x-1)-2 = x+5$.

A. -1

B. 0

C. 1

D. 2

2. Solve $2(3x-1)-(x-4)>7$.

A. $x<1$

B. $x<-1$

C. $x>-1$

D. $x>1$

3. Solve for t: $A=P+\mathrm{Pr}t$.

A. $AP-\mathrm{Pr}$

B. $A+P-\mathrm{Pr}$

C. $\dfrac{A-P}{\mathrm{Pr}}$

D. $\mathrm{Pr}(A-P)$

4. Solve: $\frac{1}{2}\left(6x-4\right)=\frac{2}{3}x$.

A. $x=-\frac{6}{7}$

B. $x=-\frac{7}{6}$

C. $x = -1$

D. $x=\frac{6}{7}$

5. **Which of the following represents the quantity 4 times the sum of 8 and an unknown subtracted from that unknown?**

A. $(4\,(8+x))-x$

B. $4(x - (8 + x))$

C. $x - (4(8 + x))$

D. $4x - (8 + x)$

6. **Which of the following demonstrates the associative property of addition?**

A. $(a+b)+c=(a+c)+(b+c)$

B. $(a+b)+c=a+(b+c)$

C. $(a+b)+c=c+(a+b)$

D. $(a+b)c=ac+bc$

7. Solve for *P:* $A = P + Prt$

A. $\dfrac{A}{1+rt}$

B. $\dfrac{A}{1-rt}$

C. $A - rt$

D. $A - 2rt$

8. Solve $\dfrac{4x-2}{3} = \dfrac{2x}{5}$.

A. $-\dfrac{5}{7}$

B. $-\dfrac{1}{7}$

C. $\dfrac{1}{7}$

D. $\dfrac{5}{7}$

9. Solve $\dfrac{3}{4}(20x-12)-7 = x+5$.

A. $-\dfrac{1}{2}$

B. -1

C. $\dfrac{1}{2}$

D. $\dfrac{3}{2}$

10. If the first term is generated when $x = 1$, what is the expression for generating the terms of {4, 6, 8, 10, 12, ...}?

A. $x + 3$

B. $5x - 1$

C. $2x - 2$

D. $2x + 2$

11. What property is exhibited here? $a + b = b + a$

A. associative property of addition

B. commutative property of addition

C. distributive property

D. zero product rule

12. Solve $-\dfrac{3}{5}(20x + 15) = \dfrac{1}{10}(20x - 90)$.

A. -2

B. -1

C. 0

D. 2

13. Solve $6(x+5) - (x-4) \leq 7x-6$.

A. $x \leq 20$

B. $x \leq -20$

C. $x \geq -20$

D. $x \geq 20$

14. Simplify $2(-1-3)^2 - \dfrac{6}{-3} - 4(2-3^0) - 7$.

A. -45

B. -4

C. 19

D. 23

15. Solve $4|x-2| = 12$.

A. -1 only

B. 5 only

C. -1 and 5

D. 1 and 5

16. Solve $\dfrac{2}{3}(2x-1) = \dfrac{5}{6}x - 4$.

A. $x = -\dfrac{20}{3}$

B. $x = -\dfrac{3}{20}$

C. $x = \dfrac{3}{20}$

D. $x = \dfrac{20}{3}$

17. Solve $4 - (2x + 3) = 5x - 9$.

A. $x = \dfrac{7}{10}$

B. $x = -\dfrac{7}{10}$

C. $x = \dfrac{10}{7}$

D. $x = -\dfrac{10}{7}$

18. What is a in the following equation? $4a - 2b = c - a$

A. $3a - 2b$

B. $2b + c$

C. $\dfrac{2b + c}{5}$

D. $c - 2b$

19. Solve $5(2x - 1) - 9x = 3 - x$.

A. -6

B. -1

C. 4

D. 7

20. Which property is exhibited by this equation? $a(x + y) = ax + ay$

A. associative property of multiplication

B. commutative property of addition

C. distributive property

D. multiplicative identity element

Answers to the Chapter Quiz

1. C

$$4(3x - 1) - 2 = x + 5$$

$$12x - 4 - 2 = x + 5$$

$$12x - 6 = x + 5$$

$$11x = 11$$

$$x = 1$$

2. D

$$2(3x - 1) - (x - 4) > 7$$

$$6x - 2 - x + 4 > 7$$

$$5x + 2 > 7$$

$$5x > 5$$

$$x > 1$$

3. **C**

$$A = P + Prt$$

$$A - P = Prt$$

$$\frac{A - P}{Pr} = t$$

4. **D**

$$\frac{1}{2}(6x - 4) = \frac{2}{3}x$$

$$3x - 2 = \frac{2}{3}x \quad \text{Multiply every term by 3.}$$

$$9x - 6 = 2x$$

$$7x = 6$$

$$x = \frac{6}{7}$$

5. **C**

"Sum" means add. Be careful to subtract the quantity from the unknown: the unknown must come first.

6. **B**

The order of the terms does not change, just the placement of the parentheses.

7. **A**

$$A = P + Prt$$

$$A = P(1 + rt)$$

$$\frac{A}{1 + rt} = P$$

8. **D**

$$\frac{4x-2}{3} = \frac{2x}{5}$$

$$5(4x - 2) = 3(2x)$$

$$20x - 10 = 6x$$

$$14x = 10$$

$$x = \frac{10}{14} = \frac{5}{7}$$

9. **D**

$$\frac{3}{4}(20x - 12) - 7 = x + 5$$

$$15x - 9 - 7 = x + 5$$

$$15x - 16 = x + 5$$

$$14x = 21$$

$$x = \frac{21}{14} = \frac{3}{2}$$

10. **D**

Try the choices to find the one that works!

11. **B**

The order of the terms switched. That is the commutative property at work!

12. C

$$-\frac{3}{5}(20x+15)=\frac{1}{10}(20x-90)$$

$$-12x - 9 = 2x - 9$$

$$-14x = 0$$

$$x = 0$$

13. D

$$6(x+5) - (x-4) \le 7x-6$$

$$6x + 30 - x + 4 \le 7x-6$$

$$5x + 34 \le 7x-6$$

$$-2x \le -40$$

Remember to flip the inequality symbol when multiplying or dividing both sides of an inequality by a negative number.

$$x \ge 20$$

14. D

$$2(-1-3)^2 - \frac{6}{-3} - 4(2-3^0) - 7$$

Parentheses first: $2(-4)^2 - \dfrac{6}{-3} - 4(2-1) - 7 = 2(-4)^2 - \dfrac{6}{-3} - 4(1) - 7$.

Exponents next: $2(16) - \dfrac{6}{-3} - 4(1) - 7$.

Multiplication and division follows: $32 - (-2) - 4 - 7$.

Finish with addition and subtraction: $32 + 2 - 4 - 7 = 34 - 4 - 7 = 30 - 7 = 23$.

15. C

$4|x - 2| = 12$

$|x - 2| = 3$

$x - 2 = 3 \quad$ and $\quad x - 2 = -3$

$x = 5 \quad\quad$ and $\quad x = -1$

16. A

$\frac{2}{3}(2x - 1) = \frac{5}{6}x - 4$

Multiply every term by 6.

$4(2x - 1) = 5x - 24$

$8x - 4 = 5x - 24$

$3x = -20$

$x = -\frac{20}{3}$

17. C

$4 - (2x + 3) = 5x - 9$

$4 - 2x - 3 = 5x - 9$

$-2x + 1 = 5x - 9$

$-7x = -10$

$x = \frac{10}{7}$

18. C

$$4a - 2b = c - a$$

$$5a - 2b = c$$

$$5a = 2b + c$$

$$a = \frac{2b + c}{5}.$$

19. C

$$5(2x - 1) - 9x = 3 - x$$
$$10x - 5 - 9x = 3 - x$$
$$x - 5 = 3 - x$$
$$2x = 8$$
$$x = 4$$

20. C

The a is distributed to both the x and the y. The final answer is the sum of those two products.

Chapter 2

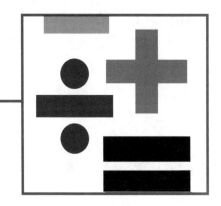

Relations and Functions

This section develops the following skills:

1. You should be able to draw and interpret graphs of relations.

2. You should understand the notation and concept of a function, find domains and ranges, and link equations to functions.

Standards

The following standards are assessed on Florida's Algebra 1 End-of-Course exam either directly or indirectly:

MA.912.A.2.3 The student describes the concept of a function, uses function notation, determines whether a given relation is a function, and links equations to functions.

MA.912.A.2.4 The student determines domain and range of a relation.

MA.912.A.2.13 The student solves real-world problems involving relations and functions.

Relations

In algebra, a **relation** is any set, or group, of ordered pairs. The symbol for "set" is { }. Any group of numbers is a relation as long as they are in the form of ordered pairs. A relation can be shown in four different ways: graph, ordered pairs, mapping diagram, or an input-output table.

Graph:

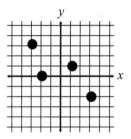

Ordered Pairs:

$$\{(-3,3), (-2,0), (1,1),$$
$$(3,-2)\}$$

Mapping Diagram:

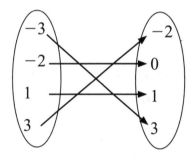

Input/Output Table

Input	Output
−3	3
−2	0
1	1
3	−2

The *domain* of the relation is the set of all *x* values.

The *range* of the relation is the set of all *y* values.

Given the relation: $\{(-2,5), (4,0), (-1,5), (100,12), (-80,74)\}$

$$\text{Domain} = \{-80, -2, -1, 4, 100\}$$

$$\text{Range} = \{0, 5, 12, 74\}$$

(Note: It is usual to list these numbers in increasing order from left to right and there is no reason to list a number more than once, even if it is found in the domain and/or range multiple times.)

Functions

A *function* is a rule that represents a relationship between two quantities, the input and the output. Each input has only one output.

x values = domain = input values

y values = range = output values

Determine if the following relation is a function:

$$\{(10, -2), (10, 15), (-28, 1), (2, 57), (3, 4)\}$$

This relation is *not* a function because the input value (10) has more than one output value (−2 and 15).

Determine if the following relation is a function:

$$\{(-3, 13), (8, -9), (5, 13), (11, 23)\}$$

This relation *is* a function because each input has only one output. Notice the output value (13) is listed twice and it is still a function.

TIP

If an x value is repeated, it is NOT a function!
If no x value is repeated, it IS a function!

Another method to determine whether or not a relation is a function is to perform the vertical line test, also known as the pencil test. If the graphed line *is* a function, then a vertical line will only touch one point on the graph at a time while moving your pencil over the graph from left to right. If your pencil touches more than one point on the graph at a given time the relation is *not* a function.

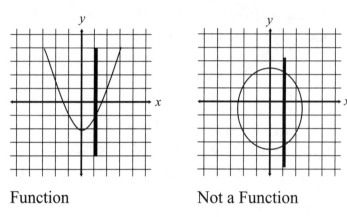

Function   Not a Function

A function is a relation, but not all relations are functions.

Exercise 1

Complete each of the following questions. Use the Tip below each question to help you choose the correct answer. When you finish, check your answers with those at the end of Chapter 2.

1. **For the graph below, answer the following questions:**

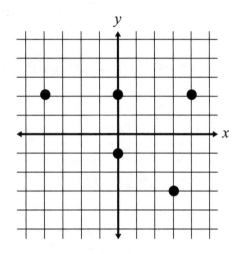

List the domain and determine if it is a function.

2. **Identify the domain and range of the following relation and determine if it is a function.**

$$\{(-1,5), (3,3), (4,3), (5,2), (7,0)\}$$

Domain:_____

Range: _____

Function: yes or no

3. **Is the following relation a function? List the ordered pairs.**

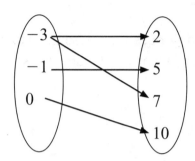

4. **Use the vertical line test to determine if the following graph is a function:**

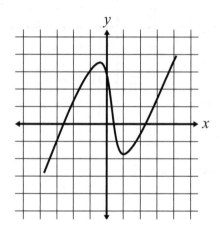

5. **Use the vertical line test to determine if the following graph is a function:**

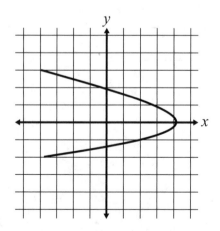

6. **List the range of the following relation:**

Input	Output
−5	3
−2	7
0	12
4	18

A. −5,−2,0,4

B. 3,7,12,18

C. −5,−2,0,3,4,7,12,18

D. −5,3,4,18

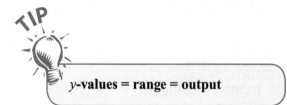

y-values = range = output

Function Notation

You can write an equation in Function Notation. The symbol for Function Notation is $f(x)$ and is read as "f of x." $f(x)$ is the output, y, for each input, x. ($f(x)$ does not mean f times x)

Example: For the function, $f(x) = -2x + 5$, evaluate for $f(-3)$.

$f(-3) = -2(-3) + 5$ Plug in -3 everywhere there is an x

$f(-3) = 6 + 5$ Multiply

$f(-3) = 11$ Simplify (Notice that we are not solving for f.)

Input   Output $(-3, 11)$

Input/Output Table

Input (x)	y=3x+2	Output (y)	Ordered Pair (x,y)
−1	y=3(−1)+2	−1	(−1,−1)
0	y=3(0)+2	2	(0,2)
1	y=3(1)+2	5	(1,5)

Function Notation

Input (x)	f(x)=3x+2	Output f(x)	Ordered Pair (x,f(x))
−1	f(−1)=3(−1)+2	−1	(−1,−1)
0	f(0)=3(0)+2	2	(0,2)
1	f(1)=3(1)+2	5	(1,5)

Here is how we can connect function notation to our everyday lives:

Imagine you are going to an amusement park with friends. Tickets are available online for $40 each plus a one-time service fee of $3. What equation models the cost of the amusement park tickets? Evaluate the function for 4 tickets.

Relate	Total Cost	Is	Cost per Ticket	Times	Number of tickets bought	Plus	Service fee
Define	C	=	40	•	t	+	3

$C = 40(t) + 3$ Write equation

$C = 40(4) + 3$ Evaluate for 4 tickets

$C = 160 + 3$ Simplify

$C = 163$ Total cost

It will cost you and your friends $163 to enjoy your day at the amusement park.

Let's try another example:

Write a function rule to model the cost per month of a cell-phone calling plan. Then, evaluate the function for the given number of minutes.

Function rule

A *function rule* is another term for writing equations. Function rules use $f(x)$ instead of $y =$.

Monthly service fee: $3.50

Rate: $.20 per minute

Minutes used: 200

Relate	Total Cost	Is	Cost per Minute	Times	Number of minutes used	Plus	Monthly Service Fee
Define	$C(m)$	=	.20	•	m	+	3.50

$C(m) = .20(m) + 3.50$ Write function rule

$C(200) = .20(200) + 3.50$ Evaluate for 200 minutes

$C(200) = 40 + 3.5$ Simplify

$C(200) = 43.5$ Your monthly bill

Exercise 2

1. Which ordered pair could not be part of a function that includes $(5,-2)$, $(6,0)$, $(-1,1)$ and $(-3,2)$?

    A. $(0,6)$

    B. $(7,-2)$

    C. $(-4,3)$

    D. $(-1,8)$

TIP

If the x value is repeated, it is NOT a function.

2. $f(x) = 16x + 2$ for $x = -2$, $f(x) =$

    A. 34

    B. -30

    C. -34

    D. 30

3. $f(x) = \dfrac{10x}{3}$ for $x = 6$, $f(x) =$

    A. 20

    B. 200

    C. 180

    D. 2

4. Write a function rule to model the cost of the cell-phone calling plan. Then, evaluate for the number of minutes used.

   Monthly service fee: $5.10

   Rate: $.15 per minute

   Minutes used: 300

5. You and your friends are going to the movies Friday night. Movie tickets cost $9.50 each. You and your friends are going to share a large popcorn that costs $5.25. Write a function rule to model the cost for the night at the movies. Evaluate the total cost for you and 4 friends.

6. Ashley, Jodie, and Kim are going to the beach for the day. They decide to rent jet skis for the afternoon. The jet skis cost $45 per hour to rent plus a one-time fee of $8 to cover the gas. If the girls rent one jet ski for 3 hours, how much will their afternoon cost?

End-of-Chapter Quiz: Relations and Functions

1. Given $f(x) = 3x - 2$, what is $f(4)$?

   A. -6

   B. 0

   C. 1

   D. 10

2. Which of the following could not be a point on the graph of a function with points $(-4,2)$, $(2,-3)$, $(6,-1)$, and $(8,-4)$?

   A. $(-4,1)$

   B. $(0,7)$

   C. $(-6,-3)$

   D. $(-2,-1)$

3. Given $f(x) = -\dfrac{2}{3}x - 6$, what is $f(-12)$?

   A. 14

   B. 2

   C. -7

   D. -14

4. Given $f(x) = -3x + 5$, what is $f(-4)$?

   A. −14

   B. 2

   C. 17

   D. 21

5. Given $f(x) = \dfrac{2}{3}x - 11$, what is $f(-6)$?

   A. 15

   B. 7

   C. −7

   D. −15

6. Vijay will have to pay for gas and lodging for his trip. Gas costs $3.05 per gallon, while the room in the hotel costs $195 per night. What is the expression that represents the total amount he will pay for gas and lodging, given that he will use g gallons and stay for n nights?

   A. $3.05n + 195g$

   B. $3.05n - 195g$

   C. $3.05g - 195n$

   D. $3.05g + 195n$

7. **Which of the following is a function?**

   A.   the line $x = -2$

   B.   a triangle

   C.   the line $y = 9$

   D.   a circle

8. **Which of the following could be a point on the graph of a function with points $(-4,2)$, $(2,-3)$, $(6,-1)$, and $(8,-4)$?**

   A. $(-4,1)$

   B. $(0,7)$

   C. $(6,-3)$

   D. $(2,1)$

9. **Given $f(x) = -\dfrac{1}{2}x + 2$, what is $f(-12)$?**

   A.   5

   B.   8

   C.   10

   D.   14

10. **Which of the following could be a function?**

   A.   a circle

   B.   a square

   C.   a triangle

   D.   a line

11. What is the range of this circle?

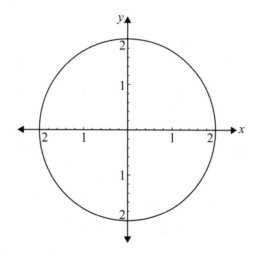

A.   All y-values from -2 to 2, including -2 and 2

B.   All x-values less than -2 and all values greater than 2

C.   All x-values between -1 and 1, excluding -1 and 1

D.   All y-values less than -2 and all values greater than 2

12. Given $f(x) = -x - 2$, what is $f(-12)$?

A.   10

B.   8

C. -12

D.   14

13. Sarra and Nell decide to spend some time at the beach. They rent a car to get to the beach. The rental costs $75 per day and $3.80 per gallon of gas used. If the pair rent the car for 3 days and use 120 gallons of gas, how much do they pay in total for the rental car?

A. $78.80

B. $68.10

C. $9,011.40

D. $681

14. **What is the range of this relation? {(−1,3),(2,5), (6,9), (7,8)}**

A. $\{-1, 2, 6, 7\}$

B. $\{-1, 2, 3, 5\}$

C. $\{-1, 2, 3, 5, 6, 7, 8, 9\}$

D. $\{3, 5, 8, 9\}$

15. **Which of the following could not be a point on the graph of a function with points (4,5), (−2,−1),(−6,10), and (8,7)?**

A. $(-4,1)$

B. $(6,11)$

C. $(4,-3)$

D. $(2,10)$

16. **What is the domain of this relation? {(−1,3), (2,5),(6,9),(7,8)}**

A. $\{-1, 2, 6, 7\}$

B. $\{-1, 2, 3, 5\}$

C. $\{-1, 2, 3, 5, 6, 7, 8, 9\}$

D. $\{3, 5, 8, 9\}$

17. **Sharla and Buck pay $6 each for movie tickets. They pay $6.40 each for snacks to munch on during the movie. How much do they pay in total for the tickets and their snacks?**

A. $12.40

B. $38.40

C. $4.80

D. $24.80

18. Which of the following is not a function?

A. the line $y = -2$

B. the line $y = 4x - 2$

C. the line $x = 9$

D. the line $y = -3x + 9$

19. Penelope and Ty go to dinner. They share a special that costs $38. They also each have a slice of pecan pie, which costs $3.50 per slice. How much do they pay, in total, for the food?

A. $83

B. $41.50

C. $45

D. $82.50

20. Given $f(x) = -\dfrac{4}{5}x + 7$, what is $f(-15)$?

A. -10

B. 8

C. 19

D. 21

Answers to the Exercises

Exercise 1

1. Domain: $-4, 0, 3, 4$; Not a Function

2. Domain: $-1, 3, 4, 5, 7$; Range: $0, 2, 3, 5$; Yes, it is a function.

3. $(-3,2)(-3,7)(-1,5)(0,10)$; Not a Function

4. Yes

5. No

6. B

Exercise 2

1. D

2. B

3. A

4. c(m)=.15m+5.10; $50.10

5. c(t)=9.50t+5.25; $52.75

6. c(h)=45h+8; $143

Answers to the Chapter Quiz

1. **D**

   $f(x) = 3x - 2$

   $f(4) = 3(4) - 2 = 12 - 2 = 10$

2. **A**

   A function cannot have two points with the same x-values and different y-values.

3. **B**

   $f(x) = -\dfrac{2}{3}x - 6$

   $f(-12) = 8 - 6 = 2$

4. **C**

   $f(x) = -3x + 5$

   $f(-4) = 12 + 5 = 17$

5. **D**

   $f(x) = \dfrac{2}{3}x - 11$

   $f(-6) = -4 - 11 = -15$

6. **D**

   Add the cost of gas and the cost of lodging. Be careful of the variables!

7. C

Choice C is the only one, since the graphs of the others fail the vertical line test. (Passing a vertical line over the graph of a function can only hit the function at 1 point.) Choice A is a vertical line, while choice C is a horizontal line.

8. B

Choice B is correct, since all of the other choices repeat an x-value, yet change the y-values. The points of functions must have only 1 y-value for each x-value.

9. B

$$f(x) = -\frac{1}{2}x + 2$$
$$f(-12) = 6 + 2 = 8$$

10. D

The graph of a function must pass the vertical line test. A horizontal line would work!

11. A

The range is the y-values.

12. A

$$f(x) = -x - 2$$

$$f(-12) = 12 - 2 = 10$$

13. D

$$75d + 3.8g = 75(3) + 3.8(120) = 225 + 456 = 681$$

14. D

The range is the *y*-values.

15. C

A function cannot have two points with the same *x*-values and different *y*-values.

16. A

The domain is the *x*-values.

17. D

$6(2) + 6.4(2) = 12 + 12.8 = 24.8$

18. C

Choice C is the answer because it is a vertical line. Hence, it fails the vertical line test. The other choices pass the vertical line test: a vertical line passing over these graphs would hit only 1 point at a time as it passes over the graph.

19. C

$38 + 3.5(2) = 38 + 7 = 45$

20. C

$$f(x) = -\frac{4}{5}x + 7$$
$$f(-15) = 12 + 7 = 19$$

Chapter 3
Quadratic Equations

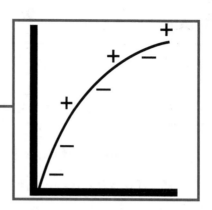

The section develops the following skills:

1. You should be able to draw graphs of quadratic functions.

2. You should know how to solve quadratic equations and solve these equations by factoring, completing the square, and by using the quadratic formula.

MA.912.A7.1   Graph quadratic equations without graphing technology.

MA.912.7.2   Solve quadratic equations over the real numbers by factoring and by using the quadratic formula.

MA.912.7.8   Use quadratic equations to solve real-world problems.

MA.912.A.1.8   Use the zero product property of real numbers in a variety of contexts to identify solutions to equations.

Quadratic Equations

A **quadratic equation** is a type of polynomial equation that has a degree of 2.

Degree represents the highest exponent in the equation. Linear equations have a degree of 1.

Standard Form: $ax^2 + bx + c = 0$, where a, b, c are real numbers and $a \neq 0$.

Properties of Quadratic Function in Standard Form

1. The graph of a quadratic equation $y = ax^2 + bx + c$ is called a parabola.

2. If $a > 0$ it opens up; If $a < 0$ it opens down

3. The axis of symmetry (AOS) is the line $x = \dfrac{-b}{2a}$ (also the x coordinate of the vertex)

The **axis of symmetry** is a line through the vertex that cuts the graph in half so that it is the same on both sides (mirror image).

4. To find the y-coordinate of the vertex substitute x values into function.

The **vertex** is the highest or the lowest point on the parabola.

5. The y-intercept is $(0, c)$

Example: $y = x^2 + 4x + 6$

1. Identify a, b, and c.

   $a = 1$, $b = 4$, and $c = 6$

2. Parabola opens up because a (1) is greater than zero.

3. Axis of symmetry $x = \dfrac{-b}{2a}$

$$x = \frac{-4}{2(1)} = \frac{-4}{2} = -2$$

$$x = -2$$

4. Vertex

The x coordinate is -2. Plug -2 into the equation to find the y value of the vertex.

$$y = (-2)^2 + 4(-2) + 6$$

$$y = 4 - 8 + 6$$

$$y = 2$$

The vertex is $(-2, 2)$

5. The y-intercept is $(0, c)$. Since $c = 6$, the y-intercept is $(0, 6)$.

   (The y-axis is shown in intervals of 2 units per box.)

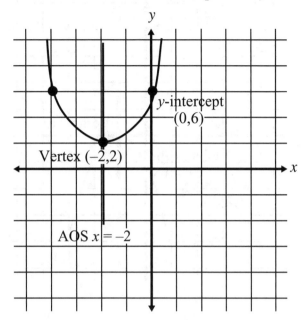

Example: $y = -x^2 + 2x - 1$

1. Identify a, b, and c.

   $a = -1, b = 2,$ and $c = -1$

2. Parabola opens down because a (-1) is less than zero.

3. Axis of symmetry $x = \dfrac{-b}{2a}$

   $$x = \frac{-2}{2(-1)} = \frac{-2}{-2} = 1$$

   $$x = 1$$

4. Vertex

The x coordinate is 1. Plug 1 into the equation to find the y value of the vertex.

$$y = -(1)^2 + 2(1) - 1$$

$$y = -1 + 2 - 1$$

$$y = 0$$

The vertex is $(1,0)$.

5. The y-intercept is $(0, c)$. Since $c = -1$, the y-intercept is $(0, -1)$.

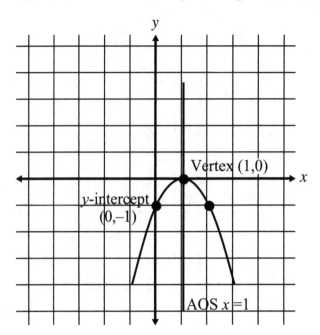

Factoring Quadratic Equations

Factoring is done to undo the **F.O.I.L.** process.

Example: Polynomial Form $x^2 + 3x + 2$

Factored Form $(x+2)(x+1)$

Greatest common factor (GCF): the largest number or variable (or combination of both) that the terms share. When you divide the GCF out of the polynomial expression, you must include the remaining terms in the parentheses.

Example: $3x - 6y$

Identify the GCF: 3

Divide each term by 3: $3(x - 2y)$

Example: $-4x^2 - 8x$

Identify the GCF: $-4x$

Divide each term by: $-4x$: $-4x(x+2)$

Example: $6x^3 + 12x^2 + 18x$

Identify the GCF: $6x$

Divide each term by $6x$: $6x(x^2+2x+3)$

Example: Polynomial Form $2x^2+4x-6$

GCF: 2

Factoring out the GCF: $2(x^2+2x-3)$ GCF (remaining terms)

Factored Form: $2(x+3)(x-1)$ (Completely factored. You will learn this next.)

Factoring Trinomials (3 terms)

$ax^2 + bx + c$

When factoring a trinomial, find two numbers that multiply to be a times c and add to be b.

Example: $x^2 + 7x + 12$

| Identify a, b, and c | $a = 1$ $b = 7$ c = 12 |
| Multiply a times c | $1(12) = 12$ |

Factors of 12	Add to be b	
$ac = 12$	$b = 7$	
1×12	$1 + 12 = 13$	$13 \neq 7$
2×6	$2 + 6 = 8$	$8 \neq 7$
3×4	$3 + 4 = 7$	$7 = 7$

Factored form: $(x+3)(x+4)$

Example: $x^2 - 10x + 24$

| Identify a, b, and c | $a = 1$ $b = -10$ $c = 24$ |
| Multiply a times c | $1(24) = 24$ |

Factors of 24	Add to be b	
$ac = 24$	$b = -10$	
1×24	$1 + 24 = 25$	$25 \neq -10$
2×12	$2 + 12 = 14$	$14 \neq -10$
3×8	$3 + 8 = 11$	$11 \neq -10$
4×6	$4 + 6 = 10$	$10 \neq -10$
-1×-24	$-1 + -24 = -25$	$-25 \neq -10$
-2×-12	$-2 + -12 = -14$	$-14 \neq -10$
-3×-8	$-3 + -8 = -11$	$-11 \neq -10$
-4×-6	$-4 + -6 = -10$	$-10 = -10$ ☆

Factored Form: $(x-4)(x-6)$

Example: $x^2 + 5x - 6$

| Identify a, b, and c | $a = 1$ | $b = 5$ | $c = -6$ |

Multiply a times c $1(-6) = -6$

Factors of -6	Add to be b	
$ac = -6$	$b = 5$	
1×-6	$1 + -6 = -5$	$-5 \neq 5$
2×-3	$2 + -3 = -1$	$-1 \neq 5$
-1×6	$-1 + 6 = 5$	$5 = 5$ ☆
-2×3	$-2 + 3 = 1$	$1 \neq 5$

Factored Form: $(x-1)(x+6)$

Example: $x^2 - x - 6$

| Identify a, b, and c | $a = 1$ | $b = -1$ | $c = -6$ |

Multiply a times c $1(-6) = -6$

Factors of -6	Add to be b	
$ac = -6$	$b = -1$	
1×-6	$1 + -6 = -5$	$-5 \neq -1$
2×-3	$2 + -3 = -1$	$-1 = -1$ ☆
-1×6	$-1 + 6 = 5$	$5 \neq -1$
-2×3	$-2 + 3 = 1$	$1 \neq -1$

Factored Form: $(x+2)(x-3)$

Example: $5x^2 + 11x + 2$

Identify a, b, and c $a = 5$ $b = 11$ $c = 2$

Multiply a times c $5(2) = 10$

Factors of 10	Add to be b	
$ac = 10$	$b = 11$	
1×10	$1 + 10 = 11$	$11 = 11$ ☆
2×5	$2 + 5 = 7$	$7 \neq 11$

Because a is greater than 1, we have an additional step. We are going to split the middle term and factor by grouping.

$5x^2 + 11x + 2$

$5x^2 + 10x + 1x + 2$ Split middle term.

$(5x^2 + 10x) + (1x + 2)$ Group terms.

$5x(x + 2) + 1(x + 2)$ Factor the GCF out of both parentheses.

$(5x + 1)(x + 2)$ Factored form.

Example: $7x^2 - 5x - 2$

Identify a, b, and c $a = 7$ $b = -5$ $c = -2$

Multiply a times c $7(-2) = -14$

Factors of -14	Add to be b	
$ac = -14$	$b = -5$	
1×-14	$1 + -14 = -13$	$-13 \neq -5$
2×-7	$2 + -7 = -5$	$-5 = -5$ ☆

-1×14 $-1 + 14 = 13$ $13 \neq -5$

-2×7 $-2 + 7 = 5$ $5 \neq -5$

$7x^2 - 5x - 2$

$7x^2 + 2x - 7x - 2$

$(7x^2 + 2x) + (-7x - 2)$

$x(7x + 2) - 1(7x + 2)$

$(x - 1)(7x + 2)$

Example: $12x^3 + 34x^2 + 10x$

Notice that every coefficient is even and every term has an x. Factor out the GCF.

$2x(6x^2 + 17x + 5)$

Identify a, b, and c $a = 6$ $b = 17$ $c = 5$

Multiply a times c $6(5) = 30$

Factors of 30	Add to be b	
$ac = 30$	$b = 17$	
1×30	$1 + 30 = 31$	$31 \neq 17$
2×15	$2 + 15 = 17$	$17 = 17$ ☆
3×10	$3 + 10 = 13$	$13 \neq 17$
5×6	$5 + 6 = 11$	$11 \neq 17$

$2x(6x^2 + 17x + 5)$

$2x(6x^2 + 2x + 15x + 5)$

$2x[(6x^2 + 2x) + (+15x + 5)]$

$2x[2x(3x + 1) + 5(3x + 1)]$

$2x(2x + 5)(3x + 1)$

Example: $9x^2 - 4$

Identify a, b, and c.	$a = 9$	$b = 0$	$c = -4$
Multiply a times c.	$9(-4) = -36$		

Factors of -36	Add to be b	
$ac = -36$	$b = 0$	
1×-36	$1 + -36 = -35$	$-35 \neq 0$
2×-18	$2 + -18 = -16$	$-16 \neq 0$
3×-12	$3 + -12 = -9$	$-9 \neq 0$
4×-9	$4 + -9 = -5$	$-5 \neq 0$
6×-6	$6 + -6 = 0$	$0 = 0$ ☆

$9x^2 - 4$

$9x^2 + 6x - 6x - 4$

$(9x^2 + 6x) + (-6x - 4)$

$3x(3x + 2) - 2(3x + 2)$

$(3x - 2)(3x + 2)$

Exercise 1

Complete each of the following questions.

1. Find the GCF and factor $18y^2 + 24y$

2. Find the GCF and factor $25x^3 + 10x^2 - 5x$

Zero Product Property

The **zero product property** is used to solve equations. In order to use the zero product property one side of the equation must be factored and the other side equal to zero.

Example:　$(x + 5)(x + 3) = 0$

$(x + 5) = 0$　$(x + 3) = 0$　　Set each factor equal to zero.

$x = -5$　　　$x = -3$　Solve for x.

This equation's solutions are -5 and -3.

Example:　$x(2x + 3)(x - 4) = 0$

$x = 0$　$(2x + 3) = 0$　　　$(x - 4) = 0$

Set each factor equal to zero including x.

$$2x = -3 \qquad x = 4$$

$$x = \frac{-3}{2}$$

This equation's solutions are 0, $\dfrac{-3}{2}$, and 4.

Example:　$2(x - 1)(3x + 4) = 0$

$2 \neq 0$　　　　$(x - 1) = 0$　　　　$(3x + 4) = 0$

$x = 1$　　　　　$3x = -4$

$$x = -\frac{4}{3}$$

This equation's solutions are 1 and $-\dfrac{4}{3}$.

Example: $5x^3 + 10x^2 = 0$

$5x^2(x + 2) = 0$

$5x^2 = 0$ $\qquad\qquad$ $(x + 2) = 0$

$x = 0$ $\qquad\qquad$ $x = -2$

This equation's solutions are 0 and -2.

Another method for solving quadratic equations is the **quadratic formula**.

Quadratic Formula $x = \dfrac{-b \pm \sqrt{b^2 - 4ac}}{2a}$

(Note: This formula will be provided for you.)

Example: $x^2 + 3x - 10 = 0$

Identify a, b, and c. $\qquad\qquad$ $a = 1$ $\qquad$ $b = 3$ $\qquad$ $c = -10$

Plug into the formula. $\qquad\qquad$ $x = \dfrac{-3 \pm \sqrt{3^2 - 4(1)(-10)}}{2(1)}$

$x = \dfrac{-3 \pm \sqrt{9 + 40}}{2}$

$x = \dfrac{-3 \pm \sqrt{49}}{2}$

$x = \dfrac{-3 \pm 7}{2}$

$x = \dfrac{-3 + 7}{2}$ $\quad$ or $\quad$ $x = \dfrac{-3 - 7}{2}$

$x = \dfrac{4}{2} = 2$ $\quad$ or $\quad$ $x = \dfrac{-10}{2} = -5$

This equation's solutions are 2 and -5.

Example: $2x^2 + 10x - 3 = 0$

$a = 2$ $b = 10$ $c = -3$

$$x = \frac{-10 \pm \sqrt{10^2 - 4(2)(-3)}}{2(2)}$$

$$x = \frac{-10 \pm \sqrt{100 - (-24)}}{4}$$

$$x = \frac{-10 \pm \sqrt{124}}{4}$$

$$x = \frac{-10 \pm 2\sqrt{31}}{4} \quad \text{or} \quad x = \frac{-5 \pm \sqrt{31}}{2}$$

Decimal answer: $x = .284$ or $x = -5.284$

Exercise 2

1. Find the GCF and factor $27y + 45y^2$.

2. Find the GCF and factor $8m^3 - 4m^2 + 24m$.

3. Factor $x^2 + 8x + 15$.

4. Factor $y^2 + 2y - 35$.

5. Factor $n^2 - 10n + 24$.

6. Factor $x^2 + 7x + 10$.

Exercise 3

1. Solve $x^2 - 5x + 6 = 0$.

2. Solve $x^2 - 11x + 19 = -5$.

3. Factor $7x^2 - 14x + 7$.

4. Factor $6y^2 - 18y - 24$.

5. Use the Quadratic Formula to solve $x^2 - 5x - 14 = 0$.

End-of-Chapter Quiz: Quadratics and Zero Product Property

1. Which of the following is the solution set to $4x^2 - 4x - 3 = 0$?

   A. $\left\{ -\dfrac{1}{2}, \dfrac{3}{2} \right\}$

   B. $\left\{ \dfrac{1}{2}, -\dfrac{3}{2} \right\}$

   C. $\left\{ \dfrac{3}{2}, \dfrac{1}{2} \right\}$

   D. $\left\{ -\dfrac{3}{2}, 2 \right\}$

2. What is the vertex of $y = 6x^2 + 12x - 1$?

   A. $\left\{ -\dfrac{1}{2}, \dfrac{3}{2} \right\}$

   B. $(-1, -7)$

   C. $(7, 1)$

   D. $(-1, -19)$

3. What is the y-intercept of $y = 6x^2 + 12x - 1$?

   A. 6

   B. 12

   C. -1

   D. 1

4. What is the axis of symmetry for $y = 6x^2 + 12x - 1$?

A. $y = -1$

B. $y = -7$

C. $x = 1$

D. $x = -1$

5. What is the complete factorization of $6x^2 + x - 1$?

A. $(3x - 1)(2x + 1)$

B. $(3x + 1)(2x + 1)$

C. $(3x - 1)(2x - 1)$

D. $(3x + 1)(2x - 1)$

6. What is the product of $(3x - 1)(3x + 1)$?

A. $6x^2 + x - 1$

B. $9x^2 + x - 1$

C. $9x^2 - 1$

D. $9x^2 + 1$

7. What are the solutions of $(x - 1)(2x + 5)(3x - 1) = 0$?

A. $\left\{1, \dfrac{5}{2}, -\dfrac{1}{3}\right\}$

B. $\left\{1, \dfrac{5}{2}, \dfrac{1}{3}\right\}$

C. $\left\{-1, -\dfrac{5}{2}, -\dfrac{1}{3}\right\}$

D. $\left\{1, -\dfrac{5}{2}, \dfrac{1}{3}\right\}$

8. Factor completely: $4x^3 + 7x^2 - 2x$.

A. $x(4x - 7)(x - 2)$

B. $x(4x - 1)(x - 2)$

C. $x(4x + 1)(x - 2)$

D. $x(4x - 1)(x + 2)$

9. What are the solutions of $x^2 + 2x - 3 = 0$?

A. $\{-3, 1\}$

B. $\{-3, -1\}$

C. $\{3, 1\}$

D. $\{3, -1\}$

10. What is the GCF of $14x^3 + 72x^2$

A. $2x$

B. $2x^2$

C. $144x^3$

D. x

11. Factor $16x^2 - 25$.

A. $(4x + 5)(4x - 5)$

B. $(16x - 5)(x + 5)$

C. $(4x - 25)(x + 1)$

D. $(4x - 1)(4x - 25)$

12. Factor $36x^2 - 49$.

A. $(6x - 49)(x + 1)$

B. $(30x - 5)(6x - 44)$

C. $(6x - 7)(6x + 7)$

D. $(6x - 40)(x + 9)$

13. What is the GCF of $42x^3 + 72x^5$

A. $2x^3$

B. $7x^5$

C. $6x^3$

D. x

14. What is the vertex of $y = 36x^2 - 49$?

A. $(0, -49)$

B. $(0, 49)$

C. $(36, 0)$

D. $(36, -49)$

15. Which of the following is a parabola that opens up?

A. $y = 4x^3 + 7x^2 - 2x$

B. $y = -4x^2 + 7x - 11$

C. $y = 4x^2 + 7x - 11$

D. $y = -4x^3 + 7x^2 - 2x$

16. What is the axis of symmetry of $y = x^2 + 2x - 5$?

A. $y = -5$

B. $x = 1$

C. $y = 5$

D. $x = -1$

17. Which of the following are characteristics of $y = x^2 + 2x - 5$?

A. y-intercept of 5 and opens down

B. x-intercept of -5 and opens down

C. y-intercept of -5 and opens up

D. y-intercept of -5 and opens down

18. Which of the following approximate the solutions to $3x^2 - 2x - 7 = 0$ to the nearest thousandth?

A. $\{-1.003, 1.003\}$

B. $\{-1.230, 1.897\}$

C. $\{1.230, -1.897\}$

D. $\{1.003, 1.987\}$

19. Factor completely: $4x^3 - 25x$.

A. $x(4x - 25)(x - 1)$

B. $x(4x + 25)(x - 1)$

C. $x(4x - 5)(x + 5)$

D. $x(2x - 5)(2x + 5)$

20. Which of the following is NOT a parabola that opens up?

A. $y - x^2 = 2x - 5$

B. $y + x^2 = 2x - 5$

C. $y - 6 = x^2 - 2x$

D. $y - x^2 - x = -5$

Answers to the Exercises

Exercise 1

1. The GCF is 6y.

    Factored form: $6y(3y + 4)$

2. The GCF is 5x.

    Factored form: $5x(5x^2 + 2x - 1)$

Exercise 2

1. The GCF is 9y.

    Factored form: $9y(3 + 5y)$

2. The GCF is 4m.

    Factored form: $4m(2m^2 - m + 6)$

3. Find two numbers that multiply to be 15 and that add to be 8.

    $(x + 5)(x + 3)$

4. Find two numbers that multiply to be –35 and that add or subtract to be 2.

    $(y + 7)(y - 5)$

5. Find two numbers that multiply to be 24 and that add or subtract to be –10.

    $(n - 4)(n - 6)$

6. Find two numbers that multiply to be 10 and add to be 7.

    $(x + 2)(x + 5)$

Exercise 3

1. Factor the trinomial. Then set each factor equal to zero and solve for x.

    $(x - 2)(x - 3) = 0$

    $x = 2$

    $x = 3$

2. First, rewrite the given equation as $x^2 - 11x + 24 = 0$.

    Factor the trinomial. Then set each factor equal to zero and solve for x.

    $(x - 3)(x - 8) = 0$

    $x = 3$

    $x = 8$

3. Find the GCF. Factor the GCF out, then factor the trinomial.

    $7(x^2 - 2x + 1) = 7(x - 1)(x - 1)$

4. Find the GCF to be 6, then factor out to get $6(y^2 - 3y - 4)$.

    Find two numbers that multiply to be –4 that add or subtract to be –3.

    $6(y - 4)(y + 1)$

5. $a = 1$ $b = -5$ $c = -14$

$$x = \frac{-(-5) \pm \sqrt{(-5)^2 - (4)(1)(-14)}}{2(1)}$$

$$= \frac{5 \pm \sqrt{25 + 56}}{2}$$

$$= \frac{5 \pm \sqrt{81}}{2}$$

$$= \frac{5 \pm 9}{2}$$

$$x = 7 \quad x = -2$$

Answers to the Chapter Quiz

1. **A**

$$4x^2 - 4x - 3 = 0$$
$$(2x + 1)(2x - 3) = 0$$
$$x = -\frac{1}{2} \quad x = \frac{3}{2}$$

2. **B**

The x-value of the vertex is $-\dfrac{b}{2a} = -\dfrac{12}{2(6)} = -\dfrac{12}{12} = -1$. Then, to find the y-value of the vertex, put x back into the original function: $y = 6x^2 + 12x - 1 = 6(-1)^2 + 12(-1) - 1 = 6 - 12 - 1 = -7$.

3. **C**

Put 0 in for x to get the y-intercept.

4. **D**

   The x-value of the vertex of this parabola is -1, from $-\dfrac{b}{2a} = -\dfrac{12}{2(6)} = -\dfrac{12}{12} = -1$.
   The axis of symmetry is the vertical line through that point.

5. **A**

   Either use trial and error to find the two factors that will multiply together to form the original expression or try all of the choices to find the one that works.

6. **C**

   $(3x-1)(3x+1) = 3x(3x+1) - 1(3x + 1) = 9x^2 + 3x - 3x - 1 = 9x^2 - 1$

7. **D**

   Set each factor equal to 0 and solve for x.

8. **D**

   $4x^3 + 7x^2 - 2x = x(4x^2 + 7x - 2) = x(4x - 1)(x + 2)$

9. **A**

   $x^2 + 2x - 3 = 0$

   $(x+3)(x-1) = 0$

   $x = -3 \quad x = 1$

10. **B**

    The GCF is the largest value that divides into each term.

11. A

This is the difference of two perfect squares. So, take the square root of each term: $4x$ and 5. These are the values in each ( ). Place a plus sign in one of the ( ) and a minus sign in the other.

12. C

This is the difference of two perfect squares. So, take the square root of each term: $6x$ and 7. Those are the values in each ( ). Place a plus sign in 1 ( ) and a minus sign in the other.

13. C

The GCF of 42 and 72 is 6. The GCF of x^3 and x^5 is x^3.

14. A

The x-value of the vertex of this parabola is 0, from $-\dfrac{b}{2a} = -\dfrac{0}{2(36)} = -\dfrac{0}{72} = 0$.

Then, to find the y-value of the vertex, put x back into the original function: $y = 36x^2 - 49 = 36(0)^2 - 49 = 0 - 49 = -49$.

15. C

Choices B and C are parabolas, since they are in the form $y = ax^2 + bx + $ c. A parabola opens up if a is positive.

16. D

The x-value of the vertex of this parabola is -1, from $-\dfrac{b}{2a} = -\dfrac{2}{2(1)} = -\dfrac{2}{2} = -1$.

The axis of symmetry is the vertical line through that point.

17. C

The parabola opens up, since a is positive. (The parabola is in the form $y = ax^2 + bx + c$.) The y-intercept is -5, since that is the result when $x=0$.

18. B

$a = 3, b = -2, c = -7$

$$x = \frac{-(-2) \pm \sqrt{(-2)^2 - 4(3)(-7)}}{2(3)}$$

$$= \frac{2 \pm \sqrt{4 + 84}}{6}$$

$$= \frac{2 \pm 9.38}{6} = 1.897 \text{ or } -1.230$$

19. D

$$4x^3 - 25x = x(4x^2 - 25) = x(2x - 5)(2x + 5)$$

This factoring began with taking out the GCF, followed by the difference of 2 perfect squares.

20. B

The choices are A: $y = x^2 + 2x - 5$, B: $y = -x^2 + 2x - 5$, C: $y = x^2 - 2x + 6$, and D: $y = x^2 + x - 5$. A parabola opens up if the a of $y = ax^2 + bx + c$ is positive. Hence, they all open up except B.

Chapter 4
Polynomials

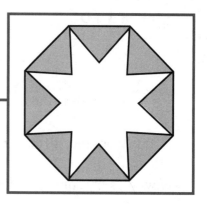

The section develops the following skills.

1. You should be able to perform operations on polynomials.
2. You should be able to factor polynomials including quadratics using special techniques.
3. You should be able to understand the relationship among a polynomial equation's factors, solutions, zeros, and x-intercepts.

The following standards are assessed on the Florida's Algebra 1 End-of-Course exam either directly or indirectly:

MA.912.A.4.1 Simplify monomials and monomial expressions using the laws of integral exponents.

MA.912.A.4.2 Add, subtract, and multiply polynomials.

MA.912.A.4.3 Factor polynomial expressions.

MA.912.A.4.4 Divide polynomials by monomials and polynomials with various techniques, including synthetic division.

Exponents

Exponents: exponents are a shortcut for writing a multiplication problem. An exponent tells you how many times to multiply a number by itself. For example:

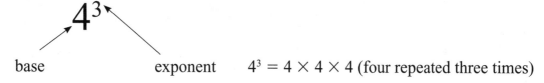

base   exponent $4^3 = 4 \times 4 \times 4$ (four repeated three times)

Base: the base is the repeated number, in this example 4 is the base.

In this example, 4 (the base) is multiplied 3 (the exponent) times.

Now let's try some problems.

a) Solve 2^3 $2 \times 2 \times 2 = 8$

b) Solve 3^5 $3 \times 3 \times 3 \times 3 \times 3 = 243$

c) Solve 5^3 $5 \times 5 \times 5 = 125$

d) Identify the base and the exponent for p^9 base $= p$ exponent $= 9$

Polynomials

Polynomials are expressions that include numbers and variables. The variables are separated by addition, subtraction, or multiplication. Division and square roots cannot be used between or with variables.

Polynomials contain more than one term.

Monomial (**"mono" means one**) has one term: $6z$ or $-2a^2$ or 16.

Binomial (**"bi" means two**) has two terms: $-4x^2 - 7$, or $11y - 3y^2$

Trinomial (**"tri" means three**) has 3 terms: $-4x^2 + 2 - 3x$, or $9y - 2y^2 + y^3$

Constant is a number with no variables

Variable is a letter representing a number: x, y, z

Degree of a polynomial

The **degree of a polynomial** is the highest exponent in a polynomial.

For example, the degree of the trinomial $-2x^3 + x^2 - 3$ has degree 3 since 3 is the highest exponent; the degree of the binomial $4x - x^2$ has degree 2 since 2 is the highest exponent.

Sometimes the first term has more than one variable. If this is the case, you must add the exponents together. In the polynomial $4a^2b^4 + 3a - 5$ the first term ($4a^2b^4$) has a degree of 6 (the sum of 2 and 4).

Examples:

$5x^2 + 28xy - 16y^2$ This triomial has a degree of 2. (Look at $5x^2$, 2 is highest exponent.)

$8x^4 + 29x^5 - 3x + 12$ Re-write the polynomial is descending order
$\qquad\qquad\qquad 29x^5 + 8x^4 - 3x + 12$ This polynomial has a degree of 5. (Look at $29x^5$)

$4x^3y^2 + 2x^2 - 3y - 5$ Look at the first term ($4x^3y^2$ add the exponents)
$\qquad\qquad\qquad$ This polynomial has a degree of 5.

For the following problems classify the polynomials by degree and number of terms. For the number of terms, use vocabulary such as *monomial, binomial, trinomial* or *polynomial*.

1. $x^4 - 3x^3 + 2x - 6$ Degree:

_____   Term:

2. $7x^2y^3$ Degree:

_____   Term:

3. $3x^2 - 5x + 10$ Degree:

_____   Term:

1. 4th degree, polynomial   2. 5th degree, monomial   3. 2nd degree trinomial

Laws of Exponents

The Laws of Exponents are as follows:

Multiplying like Bases (Add exponents): $\qquad x^2 \cdot x^5 = x^{2+5} = x^7$

Dividing like Bases (Subtract exponents): $\qquad \dfrac{x^8}{x^3} = x^{8-3} = x^5, x \neq 0$

Power raised to another Power (multiply exponents): $(x^3)^5 = x^{3 \cdot 5} = x^{15}$

Negative exponents in the numerator (bring down and make positive):

$$\frac{x^{-2}}{3} = \frac{1}{3x^2}$$

Negative exponents in the denominator (bring up and make positive):

$$\frac{4}{x^{-3}} = \frac{4x^3}{1}$$

Example:

Simplify $x^5 \cdot x^6$.

(Remember to add the exponents when multiplying **like bases**.)

$x^{5+6} = x^{11}$

The rule above works only when multiplying powers of the **same base**.

$(p^3)(r^4) = (p)(p)(p)(r)(r)(r)(r)$ This cannot be simplified.

If the bases are different but the exponents are the same, then we can simplify:

$p^3r^3 = (p)(p)(p)(r)(r)(r) = (p)(r)(p)(r)(p)(r) = (pr)(pr)(pr) = (pr)^3$

$$(p^3)(r^3) = (pr)^3$$

The laws of exponents work in both directions. If you have $(5x)^3$ you can distribute the exponent to get $(5^3)(x^3)$, and if you have $(5^3)(x^3)$, you can combine it as $(5x)^3$.

Adding and Subtracting Polynomials

This is the same concept as combining like terms. You can set up your problem one of two ways. We will do both methods and you can choose the one you like better.

Example:

(Method 1)   (Method 2)

$(2x + 5y) + (3x - 2y)$
$2x + 3x = 5x$ or
$5y + -2y = 3y$
$5x + 3y$

$$\begin{array}{r} 2x + 5y \\ +\quad 3x - 2y \\ \hline 5x + 3y \end{array}$$

Example:

(Method 1)   (Method 2)

$(-x - 12y) + (2y + 5x)$ *line up like terms*
$-x + 5x = 4x$ or
$-12y + 2y = -10y$
$4x - 10y$

$$\begin{array}{r} -x - 12y \\ +\quad 5x + 2y \\ \hline 4x - 10y \end{array}$$

Example:

(Method 1)   (Method 2)

$(6x + 4y) + (x + 10y)$
$6x + x = 7x$ or
$4y + 10y = 14y$
$7x + 14y$

$$\begin{array}{r} 6x + 4y \\ +\quad x + 10y \\ \hline 7x + 14y \end{array}$$

Example:

(Method 1)   (Method 2)

$(3x^4 + 2x^3 + 5x^2 + 3x + 2) + (-2x^4 - 6x^3 + 9x + 10)$

line up like terms

$3x^4 + -2x^4 = x^4$ or $3x^4 + 2x^3 + 5x^2 + 3x + 2$
$2x^3 + -6x^3 = -4x^3$ $+ \quad -2x^4 - 6x^3 + 0x^2 + 9x + 10$
$5x^2 + 0x^2 = 5x^2$ $\overline{\quad x^4 - 4x^3 + 5x^2 + 12x + 12}$
$3x + 9x = 12x$
$2 + 10 = 12$
$x^4 - 4x^3 + 5x^2 + 12x + 12$

Example:

(Method 1)   (Method 2)

$(-3x - 4y + 1) + (-5y + 8x)$ *line up like terms*
$-3x + 8x = 5x$ or $-3x - 4y + 1$
$-4y - 5y = -9y$ $+ \qquad 8x - 5y + 0$
$1 + 0 = 1$ $\overline{\qquad 5x - 9y + 1}$
$5x - 9y + 1$

Choose the method you like best, and remember to *watch* your signs!

Subtracting Polynomials

Subtracting polynomials is the same as adding polynomials, except we must first distribute the negative.

Example:

(Method 1)   (Method 2)

$(2x + 5) - (3x - 1)$
$(2x + 5) + (-3x + 1)$
$2x + -3x = -x$ or $2x + 5$
$5 + 1 = 6$ $+ \qquad -3x + 1$
$-x + 6$ $\overline{\qquad -x + 6}$

Example:

(Method 1)   (Method 2)

$(3x^4 + 2x^3 + 4x + 6) - (x^4 - 3x^2 + 2x + 1)$
$(3x^4 + 2x^3 + 4x + 6) + (-x^4 + 3x^2 - 2x - 1)$

line up like terms

$3x^4 + -x^4 = 2x^4$ or $3x^4 + 2x^3 + 0x^2 + 4x + 6$

$2x^3 + 0x^3 = 2x^3$ $+ \quad -x^4 + 0x^3 + 3x^2 - 2x - 1$

$0x^2 + 3x^2 = 3x^2$ $\overline{\qquad\quad 2x^4 + 2x^3 + 3x^2 + 2x + 5}$

$4x + -2x = 2x$

$6 + -1 = 5$

$2x^4 + 2x^3 + 3x^2 + 2x + 5$

Example:

(Method 1)   (Method 2)

$-(x + 5) + (3x - 2)$
$(-x - 5) + (3x - 2)$
$-x + 3x = 2x$ or $-x - 5$
$-5 + -2 = -7$ $+ \quad\; 3x - 2$
$2x - 7$ $\overline{\qquad\; 2x - 7}$

Here's what you might consider a "challenge problem."

$(2x^3 + 3x + 8) + (4x^3 - 3x^2 + 2x - 2) - (3x^3 + 5x^2 + 2x)$
$(2x^3 + 3x + 8) + (4x^3 - 3x^2 + 2x - 2) + (-3x^3 - 5x^2 - 2x)$

line up like terms

$2x^3 + 4x^3 - 3x^3 = 3x^3$ or $2x^3 + 0x^2 + 3x + 8$

$0x^2 + -3x^2 - 5x^2 = -8x^2$ $4x^3 - 3x^2 + 2x - 2$

$3x + 2x - 2x = 3x$ $+ \quad -3x^3 - 5x^2 - 2x + 0$

$8 + -2 + 0 = 6$ $\overline{\qquad\; 3x^3 - 8x^2 + 3x + 6}$

$3x^3 - 8x^2 + 3x + 6$

Zero Exponent

The zero exponent refers to the construct that *any number* (except zero) raised to the zero power is always 1.

$x^0 = 1 \quad x \neq 0$

$5^0 = 1$

0^0 is undefined

Multiplying Monomials

When multiplying monomials, follow these steps:

Step 1: Multiply the coefficients (numbers in front of variables)

Step 2: Multiply variables with the same base

Step 3: Simplify

Example: $(5x^3y^2)(4xy^3)$

$5 \cdot 4 = 20$

$x^3 \cdot x = x^{3+1} = x^4$

$y^2 \cdot y^3 = y^{2+3} = y^5$

$20x^4y^5$

Example: $(-2a^4b^3c)(4a^2bc^3)$

$-2 \cdot 4 = -8$

$a^4 \cdot a^2 = a^6$

$b^3 \cdot b = b^4$

$c \cdot c^3 = c^4$

$-8a^6b^4c^4$

Example: $(3x^2)^3(4xy^3)$

$3^3 \cdot x^{2 \cdot 3} = 27x^6$ First monomial: raise factor to the 3rd power

$(27x^6)(4xy^3)$ Rewrite problem

$27 \cdot 4 = 108$

$x^6 \cdot x = x^7$

$1 \cdot y^3 = y^3$

$108x^7y^3$

Example: $(5a^3b^2c)^3(5a^4)$

$5^3 = 125$

$(a^3)^3 = a^9$

$(b^2)^3 = b^6$

$(c)^3 = c^3$

$(125a^9b^6c^3)(5a^4)$

$625a^{13}b^6c^3$

Exercise 1

Complete each of the following questions.

1. Simplify $(8x^3y^5)(-2x^2y^4)$

2. Simplify $(5x^4)^2(3x^{-1}y)$

3. Simplify $(2ab^3c^2)^3(5a^5)$

4. Simplify $\dfrac{2x^3}{4x^2}$

5. Simplify $\dfrac{18a^9}{-3a^{10}}$

6. Simplify $\left(\dfrac{p^4}{p^3}\right)^4$

7. Simplify $\left(\dfrac{p^3q^5r^7}{p^4q^6r^7}\right)^2$

Multiplying Polynomials

Multiplying polynomials requires the use of the distributive property. All you need to do is to multiply each term in one polynomial by each term on the other polynomial.

Example:

$3x(x + 3xy) =$

$3x^2 + 9x^2y$

Example:

$(2x^2 - x)(3y) =$

$6x^2y - 3xy$

Using the FOIL Method to multiply two binomials

First   Last

$(a+b)(c+d)$

Inner

Outer

First		**Outer**		**Inner**		**Last**
ac	$+$	ad	$+$	bc	$+$	bd

Example:

$(x+3)(x^2-2)$

$x \cdot x^2 + x \cdot -2 + 3 \cdot x^2 + 3 \cdot -2$

$x^3 - 2x + 3x^2 - 6$

$x^3 + 3x^2 - 2x - 6$

Example:

$(5x-6)(3xy+4)$

$5x \cdot 3xy + 5x \cdot 4 + -6 \cdot 3xy + -6 \cdot 4$

$15x^2y + 20x - 18xy - 24$

$15x^2y - 18xy + 20x - 24$

Example:

$(x+2)(4x^2y+4y+3x)$

$x \cdot 4x^2y + x \cdot 4y + x \cdot 3x + 2 \cdot 4x^2y + 2 \cdot 4y + 2 \cdot 3x$

$4x^3y + 4xy + 3x^2 + 8x^2y + 8y + 6x$

$4x^3y + 8x^2y + 4xy + 3x^2 + 8y + 6x$

Example:

$(x+2y)(3x+4y-5)$

$x \cdot 3x + x \cdot 4y + x \cdot -5 + 2y \cdot 3x + 2y \cdot 4y + 2y \cdot -5$

$3x^2 + 4xy - 5x + 6xy + 8y^2 - 10y$

$3x^2 + 10xy - 5x + 8y^2 - 10y$

Dividing Polynomials

When dividing polynomials, divide by factoring.

Example:

$$\frac{x^2 + 4x + 3}{x^2 - 4x - 5}$$

Factor the top (numerator) and bottom (denominator).

$$\frac{\cancel{(x+1)}(x+3)}{\cancel{(x+1)}(x-5)}$$ Cross out factors that are common (once on top, once on bottom)

$$= \frac{x+3}{x-5}$$ Simplified

Example:

$$\frac{x^2 - x - 6}{x^2 - 3x}$$

Factor the top (numerator) and bottom (denominator).

$$\frac{\cancel{(x-3)}(x+2)}{x\cancel{(x-3)}}$$ Cross out common factors.

$$= \frac{x+2}{x}$$

Divide using synthetic division.

Example:

$(x^2 - 13x - 48) \div (x + 3)$

Steps:

1. Reverse the sign of the divisor $(x + 3)$.

2. Write the coefficients of the dividend making sure every spot is accounted for from the highest exponent down.

3. Bring down first term.

4. Multiply # in box by the # below the line number you brought down and place this product under the second coefficient of the dividend.

5. Add this product to the number above it and place the answer below the line.

6. Repeat steps 4 and 5 until you are done.

7. The numbers below the line represent the coefficients of the answer. The last number on the right represents the remainder.

Since the numbers are under the line are $1, -16, 0$, the answer is $1x - 16$. The zero remainder means that the divisor divided evenly into the dividend.

Check: $(x + 3)(x - 16)$
$x^2 - 16x + 3x - 48$
$x^2 - 13x - 48$

Example:

$(x^3 - 5x^2 - 7x + 25) \div (x - 5)$

$$
\begin{array}{r|rrrr}
5 & 1 & -5 & -7 & 25 \\
+ & & 5 & 0 & -35 \\
\hline
& 1 & 0 & -7 & \boxed{-10}
\end{array}
$$

$= x^2 + 0x - 7 \quad R - 10$

$= x^2 - 7 \quad R - 10$

Example:

$(x^3 - 57x + 56) \div (x + 8)$

*Remember every spot *must* be accounted for; therefore, we need to plug in a 0 for the "x^2" spot.

$$
\begin{array}{r|rrrr}
-8 & 1 & 0 & -57 & 56 \\
+ & & -8 & 64 & -56 \\
\hline
& 1 & -8 & 7 & \boxed{0}
\end{array}
$$

$= x^2 - 8x + 7$

Exercise 2

Complete each of the following questions.

1. **Using synthetic division:** $(x^4 - 6x^2 - 20) \div (x - 4)$

2. **Using synthetic division:** $(2x^3 - 3x^2 - 5x) \div (x + 2)$

3. **Simplify:** $\dfrac{x^2 - 3x - 10}{x^2 - 2x - 15}$

4. **Simplify:** $\dfrac{x^2 + 6x}{x^2 + 2x - 24}$

5. **Simplify:** $(3x^2 + 10x - 8) + (9x^2 - 10x)$

6. **Simplify:** $(4s^4 + 5s^2 - 2) - (6s + 3s^2 + 5)$

7. **Simplify:** $6x^2(x - 3y)$

8. **Simplify:** $(8x + 3)(-5xy - 2)$

End-of-Chapter Quiz: Polynomials

1. Simplify: $(4x^2 - 8x + 9) - (6x^2 - 7x - 3)$.

A. $-2x^2 - 15x + 6$

B. $-2x^2 - x + 6$

C. $-2x^2 - x + 12$

D. $-2x^2 - x - 12$

2. Simplify: $(4x - 2y - 6) - (3y + 10) - 2y + 1$.

A. $4x - 7y - 17$

B. $x - 2y - 17$

C. $4x - 7y + 5$

D. $4x - 7y - 15$

3. $(3x - 8)(x - 4) =$

A. $3x^2 - 20x + 32$

B. $3x^2 + 20x + 32$

C. $3x^2 + 20x - 32$

D. $3x^2 - 4x + 32$

4. $\dfrac{12x^2 - 9x}{3x} =$

A. $9x + 3$

B. $9x - 3$

C. $4x - 3$

D. $4x + 3$

5. $(3x - 8)^2 =$

A. $9x^2 - 64$

B. $9x^2 + 64$

C. $9x^2 - 48x - 64$

D. $9x^2 - 48x + 64$

6. Factor completely: $12x^3y^2 + 22x^2y^5 - 20xy$.

A. $2xy$

B. $2xy(6x^2y + 11xy^4 - 10)$

C. $2xy(10x^2y + 20xy^4 - 18)$

D. $2xy(10x^2y - 20xy^4 + 18)$

7. Simplify: $2(4x^2 - 8x + 9) - 3(6x^2 - 7x - 3) + (x - 1)$.

A. $-10x^2 - 6x - 10$

B. $-10x^2 + 6x + 26$

C. $-10x^2 + 6x + 16$

D. $2x^2 + 6x + 26$

8. Simplify: $(4x - 2y - 6) - (3x - y - 10) - (7x - 2)$.

A. $-6x - y + 6$

B. $6x - y - 6$

C. $6x - y + 6$

D. $-6x - 3y - 18$

9. $\dfrac{50x^{10}y^2z^6 - 25x^4y^8z^2 + 35x^2y^7z}{5x^2yz} =$

A. $10x^8yz^6 - 5x^2y^8z + 7y^7$

B. $45x^8yz^5 - 20x^2y^8z + 30y^7$

C. $45x^7yz^5 - 20x^2y^7z + 30y^6$

D. $10x^8yz^5 - 5x^2y^7z + 7y^6$

10. $(x - 1)(x + 1) =$

A. $x^2 - 2x + 1$

B. $x^2 - 2x - 1$

C. $x^2 + 1$

D. $x^2 - 1$

11. Factor completely: $4x^3y^6 + 21x^2y - 35xz$.

A. $x(4x^2y^6 + 21xy + 35z)$

B. $x(4x^2y^6 + 21xy - 35z)$

C. $x(4x^3y^6 + 21x^3y - 35xz)$

D. $-10(x^3y^6 + 21x^2y - xz)$

12. Simplify: $(6x^2 - 8x + 9) - (x^2 - 3) - 7x + 9$.

A. $5x^2 - 18x + 15$

B. $5x^2 - 18x - 15$

C. $5x^2 - 12x + 15$

D. $5x^2 - 15x + 21$

13. $(3x - 7)(3x + 7) =$

A. $6x^2 - 49$

B. $6x^2 + 49$

C. $9x^2 + 49$

D. $9x^2 - 49$

14. $(5x^2 - 3y)(4x + 7) =$

A. $20x^3 + 12x^2 - 12xy + 21y$

B. $9x^3 + 12x^2 - 7xy + 21y$

C. $20x^3 + 35x^2 - 12xy - 21y$

D. $9x^3 + 12x^2 - 7xy - 21y$

15. $\dfrac{10x^2y^3 - 25x^4y^8 - 5x^2y}{5x^2y} =$

A. $2y^2 - 5x^2y^8$

B. $2y^2 - 5x^2y^7 - 1$

C. $5y^2 - 20x^2 - 10$

D. $5y^2 - 20x^2y^7 + 1$

16. $\dfrac{29x^2yz + 31xy^5z^7 - 19xyz}{xyz} =$

A. $29x + 31y^5z^7$

B. $29x + 31y^4z^6 - 19$

C. $29xyz + 31x^4 - 19z$

D. $29x^2 + 31y^4z^7 - 19$

17. Simplify: $(5x - 7y + 9) + (x - y - 1)$.

A. $4x - 8y + 10$

B. $6x - 7y + 8$

C. $6x - 8y + 8$

D. $4x - 8y + 8$

18. $(4x - 3)^2 =$

A. $8x^2 - 24x - 9$

B. $8x^2 + 24x + 9$

C. $16x^2 - 24x - 9$

D. $16x^2 - 24x + 9$

19. Simplify: $7(x^2 - x + 2) - 3(6x^2 - 7x) - 10.$

A. $-11x^2 + 14x + 4$

B. $-11x^2 - 14x + 4$

C. $x^2 - 14x - 4$

D. $x^2 - 10$

20. Factor completely: $12x^3 + 22x^2 - 20x.$

A. $2x(6x^2 + 11x - 10)$

B. $2x(6x^3 + 11x^2 - 20x)$

C. $2x(10x^2 + 20x - 18x)$

D. $2x(3x - 2)(2x + 5)$

Answers to the Exercises

Exercise 1

1. $-16x^{3+2}y^{5+4}$

    $-16x^5y^9$

2. $(25x^8)(3x^{-1}y)$

    $75x^{8-1}y$

    $75x^7y$

3. $(8a^3b^9c^6)(5a^5)$

    $40a^{3+5}b^9c^6$

    $40a^8b^9c^6$

4. $\dfrac{1}{2}x^{3-2}$

    $\dfrac{1x}{2}$ or $\dfrac{x}{2}$

5. $\dfrac{-6}{1} \cdot a^{9-10}$

    $\dfrac{-6}{1} \cdot a^{-1} = \dfrac{-6}{1} \cdot \dfrac{1}{a} = \dfrac{-6}{a}$

6. $(p^{4-3})^4 = (p)^4 = p^4$

7. $(p^{3-4}q^{5-6}r^{7-7})^2$

$(p^{-1}q^{-1}r^0)^2$

$p^{-2}q^{-2} = \dfrac{1}{p^2q^2}$

Exercise 2

1. $\begin{array}{r|rrrrr} 4 & 1 & 0 & -6 & 0 & -20 \\ & & 4 & 16 & 40 & 160 \\ \hline & 1 & 4 & 10 & 40 & 140 \end{array}$

    $x^3 + 4x^2 + 10x + 40$ *remainder* **140**

2. $(2x^3 - 3x^2 - 5x) \div (x + 2)$

    $\begin{array}{r|rrrr} -2 & 2 & -3 & -5 & 0 \\ & & -4 & 14 & -18 \\ \hline & 2 & -7 & 9 & -18 \end{array}$

    $2x^2 - 7x + 9$ *remainder* **−18**

3. $\dfrac{(x-5)(x+2)}{(x-5)(x+3)} =$

    $\dfrac{(x-5)(x+2)}{(x-5)(x+3)} = \dfrac{(x+2)}{(x+3)}$

4. $\dfrac{x(x+6)}{(x+6)(x-4)} =$

    $\dfrac{x(x+6)}{(x+6)(x-4)} = \dfrac{x}{x-4}$

5. $3x^2 + 10x - 8$

 $\underline{9x^2 - 10x + 0}$

 $12x^2 + 0x - 8 = 12x^2 - 8$

6. $4s^4 + 5s^2 + 0s - 2$

 $\underline{ -3s^2 - 6s - 5}$

 $4s^4 + 2s^2 - 6s - 7$

7. $6x^3 - 18x^2\,y$

8. $-40x^2\,y - 16x - 15xy - 6$

 $-40x^2\,y - 15xy - 16x - 6$

Answers to the Chapter Quiz

1. C

$(4x^2 - 8x + 9) - (6x^2 - 7x - 3)$

$= 4x^2 - 8x + 9 - 6x^2 + 7x + 3 = -2x^2 - x + 12$

2. D

$(4x - 2y - 6) - (3y + 10) - 2y + 1$

$4x - 2y - 6 - 3y - 10 - 2y + 1 = 4x - 7y - 15$

3. A

$(3x-8)(x-4) = 3x(x-4) - 8(x-4) = 3x^2 - 12x - 8x + 32 = 3x^2 - 20x + 32$

4. C

$\dfrac{12x^2 - 9x}{3x} = \dfrac{12x^2}{3x} - \dfrac{9x}{3x} = 4x - 3$

5. D

$(3x-8)^2 = (3x-8)(3x-8) = 3x(3x-8) - 8(3x-8) = 9x^2 - 24x - 24x + 64$

$= 9x^2 - 48x + 64$

6. B

$12x^3y^2 + 22x^2y^5 - 20xy = 2xy(6x^2y + 11xy^4 - 10)$

7. **B**

$$2\left(4x^2 - 8x + 9\right) - 3\left(6x^2 - 7x - 3\right) + \left(x - 1\right)$$
$$= 8x^2 - 16x + 18 - 18x^2 + 21x + 9 + x - 1 = -10x^2 + 6x + 26$$

8. **A**

$$\left(4x - 2y - 6\right) - \left(3x - y - 10\right) - \left(7x - 2\right)$$
$$= 4x - 2y - 6 - 3x + y + 10 - 7x + 2 = -6x - y + 6$$

9. **D**

$$\frac{50x^{10}y^2z^6 - 25x^4y^8z^2 + 35x^2y^7z}{5x^2yz} = \frac{50x^{10}y^2z^6}{5x^2yz} - \frac{25x^4y^8z^2}{5x^2yz} + \frac{35x^2y^7z}{5x^2yz}$$
$$= 10x^8yz^5 - 5x^2y^7z + 7y^6$$

10. **D**

$$\left(x - 1\right)\left(x + 1\right) = x\left(x + 1\right) - 1\left(x + 1\right) = x^2 + x - x - 1 = x^2 - 1$$

11. **B**

$$4x^3y^6 + 21x^2y - 35xz = x\left(4x^2y^6 + 21xy - 35z\right)$$

12. **D**

$$\left(6x^2 - 8x + 9\right) - \left(x^2 - 3\right) - 7x + 9 = 6x^2 - 8x + 9 - x^2 + 3 - 7x + 9$$
$$= 5x^2 - 15x + 21$$

13. D

$$(3x-7)(3x+7) = 3x(3x+7) - 7(3x+7) = 9x^2 + 21x - 21x - 49 = 9x^2 - 49$$

14. C

$$(5x^2 - 3y)(4x+7) = 5x^2(4x+7) - 3y(4x+7) = 20x^3 + 35x^2 - 12xy - 21y$$

15. B

$$\frac{10x^2 y^3 - 25x^4 y^8 - 5x^2 y}{5x^2 y} = \frac{10x^2 y^3}{5x^2 y} - \frac{25x^4 y^8}{5x^2 y} - \frac{5x^2 y}{5x^2 y} = 2y^2 - 5x^2 y^7 - 1$$

16. B

$$\frac{29x^2 yz + 31xy^5 z^7 - 19xyz}{xyz} = \frac{29x^2 yz}{xyz} + \frac{31xy^5 z^7}{xyz} - \frac{19xyz}{xyz} = 29x + 31y^4 z^6 - 19$$

17. C

$$(5x - 7y + 9) + (x - y - 1) = 5x - 7y + 9 + x - y - 1 = 6x - 8y + 8$$

18. D

$$(4x-3)^2 = (4x-3)(4x-3) = 4x(4x-3) - 3(4x-3) = 16x^2 - 12x - 12x + 9$$
$$= 16x^2 - 24x + 9$$

19. A

$$7\left(x^2 - x + 2\right) - 3\left(6x^2 - 7x\right) - 10 = 7x^2 - 7x + 14 - 18x^2 + 21x - 10$$
$$= -11x^2 + 14x + 4$$

20. D

$$12x^3 + 22x^2 - 20x = 2x\left(6x^2 + 11x - 10\right) = 2x\left(3x - 2\right)\left(2x + 5\right)$$

Chapter 5

Ratios and Proportions

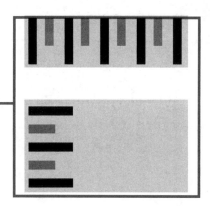

The section develops the following skills:

1. You should be able to simplify rational expressions and

2. Solve rational equations using what has been learned about factoring polynomials.

The following standards are assessed on the Florida's Algebra 1 End-of-Course exam either directly or indirectly:

MA.912.A.5.1   Simplify algebraic ratios.

MA.912.A.5.4   Solve algebraic proportions.

Ratios

A **ratio** is the comparison of two quantities. The ratio of a number a to a number b can be denoted by any of the following

a to b both a and b are integers; $b \neq 0$

$a:b$

$\dfrac{a}{b}$

When comparing two quantities in fraction form, be sure to always simplify/reduce your fractions.

Example:

Express the following ratio as a fraction: 10 weeks to 12 weeks

$\dfrac{10}{12}$ Simplify by dividing both 10 and 12 by 2. $= \dfrac{5}{6}$

Example:

Express the following ratio as a fraction: 8 days to 1 week

First, convert 1 week to 7 days.

They must have the same units.

$\dfrac{8\,days}{7\,days} = \dfrac{8}{7}$

Sometimes you will be asked to simplify a ratio that contains a fraction.

Example:

Write 3 to $4\dfrac{1}{3}$ as a ratio in fraction form.

3 to $\dfrac{13}{3}$ **Step 1:** Write $4\dfrac{1}{3}$ as an improper fraction.

$$4 \cdot 3 + 1 = 13 => \dfrac{13}{3}$$

$\dfrac{3}{\dfrac{13}{3}}$ **Step 2:** Set up the ratio in fractional form.

$\dfrac{3}{1} \div \dfrac{13}{3}$ **Step 3:** Simplify the complex fraction.

$\dfrac{3}{1} \cdot \dfrac{3}{13}$ **Step 4:** <u>K</u>eep the first fraction.
                            <u>F</u>lip the 2nd fraction upside down.
                            <u>C</u>hange sign to multiplication.

$\dfrac{9}{13}$ **Step 5:** Simplify.

Example:

Write the given ratio in fractional form: $\dfrac{25}{2}$ to 8.

(Notice this time the fraction is already written as an improper fraction.)

$\dfrac{\dfrac{25}{2}}{8}$ **Step 1:** Set up the ratio in fractional form.

$\dfrac{25}{2} \div \dfrac{8}{1}$ **Step 2:** Simplify the complex fraction.

$\dfrac{25}{2} \cdot \dfrac{1}{8}$ **Step 3:** <u>K</u>eep the first fraction.
                            <u>F</u>lip the 2nd fraction upside down.
                            <u>C</u>hange sign to multiplication.

$\dfrac{25}{16}$ **Step 4:** Simplify.

Rational Expressions

A **rational expression** is the quotient of two polynomials.

Example:

Simplify the following ratio: $\dfrac{8xy}{12xy}$

$$\frac{8xy}{12xy} \;=\; \frac{2 \cdot 2 \cdot 2 \cdot x \cdot y}{2 \cdot 2 \cdot 3 \cdot x \cdot y} \;=\; \frac{2 \cdot 2 \cdot 2 \cdot x \cdot y}{2 \cdot 2 \cdot 3 \cdot x \cdot y} \;=\; \frac{2}{3}$$

Factor numerator and denominator

Cross out commons

Example:

Simplify the following ratio: $\dfrac{5xy^2}{25x^2y}$

$$\frac{5xy^2}{25x^2y} \;=\; \frac{5 \cdot x \cdot y \cdot y}{5 \cdot 5 \cdot x \cdot x \cdot y}$$

What is left once you cross out the commons?

$$=\; \frac{y}{5x} \quad \text{Simplified}$$

Example:

Simplify the following ratio: $\dfrac{27a^3bc^2}{36ab^3c^2}$

$$\frac{27a^3bc^2}{36ab^3c^2} \;=\; \frac{3 \cdot 9 \cdot a \cdot a \cdot a \cdot b \cdot c \cdot c}{4 \cdot 9 \cdot a \cdot b \cdot b \cdot b \cdot c \cdot c}$$

What is left once you cross out the commons?

$$=\; \frac{3a^2}{4b_2^2} \quad \text{Simplified}$$

Exercise 1

Complete each of the following questions.

1. **Express the ratio as a fraction in simplest form:**

   6 to 24

2. **Express the ratio as a fraction in simplest form:**

   10 to 62

3. **Express the ratio as a fraction in simplest form:**

   3 yards to 5 feet   (3 feet = 1 yard)

4. **In Kim's math class there are 12 girls and 16 boys. Find the ratio of girls to boys.**

5. **Mrs. Carleton has 8 grandchildren and 4 children. Find the fraction that best compares children to grandchildren.**

6. **Ashley's softball team won 17 games and lost 3 games. What is the ratio of losses to wins?**

7. **Express the ratio of the first number to the second number in simplest form:**

   $3.40 to $2.10

Proportions

A **proportion** is a mathematical sentence that states two ratios are equal to each other.

There are two ways to write proportions.

$$3:5 = 15:25 \quad \text{or} \quad \frac{3}{5} = \frac{15}{25}$$

The way the proportion is read "3 is to 5 as 15 is to 25."

There are extremes and means in proportions.

$$\frac{a}{b} = \frac{c}{d}$$

Extremes: a and d

Means: b and c

We use the multiplication property of equality to show that the product of the extremes ($a \cdot d$) is equal to the product of the means ($b \cdot c$).

Algebraic proportions

Sometimes variables are used in proportions, and this is called an **algebraic proportion**.

$$n:3 = 6:18 \quad \text{or} \quad \frac{n}{3} = \frac{6}{18}$$

Example:

Solve for x.

Cross multiply and solve for x.

$$\frac{6}{49} = \frac{2}{x}$$

$6 \cdot x = 2 \cdot 49$ Cross multiply.

$6x = 98$ Divide by 6.

$x = \dfrac{98}{6}$ or $\dfrac{49}{3}$

Example:

Solve for x.

$$\dfrac{5x}{10} = \dfrac{6}{3}$$ Cross multiply and solve for x.

$5x \cdot 3 = 6 \cdot 10$ Cross multiply.

$15x = 60$ Divide by 15.

$x = 4$

Example:

Solve for x.

$\dfrac{4}{x-5} = \dfrac{2}{3}$ Cross multiply and solve for x.

$4 \cdot 3 = 2 \cdot (x-5)$ Cross multiply and then distribute

$12 = 2x - 10$ Add 10 to both sides

$22 = 2x$ Divide by 2

$11 = x$ or $x = 11$

Example:

Solve for x.

$\dfrac{3}{x+5} = \dfrac{-4}{x-2}$ Cross multiply and solve for x.

$3(x-2) = -4(x+5)$ Be careful with distributing a negative.

$3x - 6 = -4x - 20$ Move x's to the left.

$7x - 6 = -20$ Move constants to the right.

$7x = -14$ Divide by 7.

$x = -2$

Example:

Solve for x.

$\dfrac{x+1}{7} = \dfrac{x+2}{3}$ Cross multiply and solve for x.

$3(x + 1) = 7(x + 2)$ Distribute.

$3x + 3 = 7x + 14$ Move x's to the right so they are positive.

$3 = 4x + 14$ Move constants to the left (subtract 14).

$-11 = 4x$ Divide by 4.

$$\dfrac{-11}{4} = x \quad \text{or} \quad x = \dfrac{-11}{4}$$

Exercise 2

Complete each of the following questions.

1. **Solve the proportion:**

   $$\frac{2}{5} = \frac{14}{z}$$

2. **Solve the proportion:**

   $$\frac{2y}{7} = \frac{-3}{9}$$

3. **Solve the proportion:**

   $$\frac{-3}{-2} = \frac{x+8}{-x+17}$$

4. **Solve the proportion:**

   $$\frac{4}{5y} = \frac{8}{10}$$

5. **Ashley reads 40 pages in 50 minutes. How many pages should she be able to read in 90 minutes? Set up and solve the proportion.**

6. **Jodie takes inventory of her closet and finds that she has 10 shirts for every 6 pairs of shorts. If she has 24 pairs of shorts how many shirts will Jodie have? Set up and solve the proportion.**

End-of-Chapter Quiz: Rational Expressions and Equations

1. Express the ratio 14 to 21 as a fraction in simplest form.

   A. $\dfrac{2}{3}$

   B. $\dfrac{3}{2}$

   C. $\dfrac{14}{21}$

   D. $\dfrac{21}{14}$

2. Jourdan has 16 female friends and 18 male friends. What is the ratio, in simplest form, of her male friends to female friends?

   A. $\dfrac{2}{1}$

   B. $\dfrac{9}{8}$

   C. $\dfrac{8}{9}$

   D. $\dfrac{1}{2}$

3. Solve the proportion $\dfrac{10}{21} = \dfrac{2x}{3x-6}$.

   A. $x = 5$

   B. $x = -5$

   C. $x = -\dfrac{5}{6}$

   D. $x = \dfrac{5}{6}$

4. Hank lost 5 of his baseball games and won 11 of them. What is the ratio of his wins to his losses?

A. $\dfrac{5}{11}$

B. $\dfrac{5}{16}$

C. $\dfrac{11}{16}$

D. $\dfrac{11}{5}$

5. Kendra writes 20 pages in 50 minutes. How many minutes should it take her to write 60 pages?

A. 90

B. 60

C. 150

D. 2.5

6. Denver has 17 golf balls and 11 hockey pucks. What is the ratio of hockey pucks to golf balls?

A. 17 to 11

B. 11 to 28

C. 17 to 28

D. 11 to 17

7. **Given 12 inches = 1 foot, express the ratio of 5 feet to 3 inches in simplest form.**

   A. 1 to 20

   B. 20 to 1

   C. 5 to 3

   D. 3 to 5

8. **Sandri has 8 pens for every 6 notebooks that he has. If he has 21 notebooks, how many pens does he have?**

   A. 90

   B. 60

   C. 28

   D. 2.5

9. **Express the ratio 15 to 42 as a fraction in simplest form.**

   A. $\dfrac{1}{27}$

   B. $\dfrac{5}{14}$

   C. $\dfrac{3}{14}$

   D. $\dfrac{27}{1}$

10. **What is the simplified ratio of 3 hours to 27 minutes, given 60 minutes = 1 hour?**

   A. $\dfrac{1}{9}$

   B. $\dfrac{9}{1}$

   C. $\dfrac{3}{20}$

   D. $\dfrac{20}{3}$

11. **Theo's volleyball team has a ratio of 6 gals for every 7 guys. If the team has 21 guys on it, how many gals are on the team?**

   A. 18

   B. 20

   C. 2

   D. 22

12. **What is the simplified ratio of 24 to 40?**

   A. $\dfrac{1}{16}$

   B. $\dfrac{2}{5}$

   C. $\dfrac{16}{1}$

   D. $\dfrac{3}{5}$

13. What is the simplified ratio of 15 inches to 4 feet, given 12 inches = 1 foot?

   A. $\dfrac{12}{1}$

   B. $\dfrac{15}{4}$

   C. $\dfrac{5}{16}$

   D. $\dfrac{45}{1}$

14. Mack edits 21 pages in 35 minutes. How many pages should he be able to edit in 20 minutes?

   A. 6

   B. 10

   C. 12

   D. 33.3

15. Isaac has 16 dimes and 24 nickels. What is the simplified ratio of his nickels to his dimes?

   A. $\dfrac{3}{2}$

   B. $\dfrac{1}{1}$

   C. $\dfrac{1}{7}$

   D. $\dfrac{2}{7}$

16. Express the ratio 14 to 49 as a fraction in simplest form.

A. $\dfrac{7}{2}$

B. $\dfrac{1}{1}$

C. $\dfrac{1}{7}$

D. $\dfrac{2}{7}$

17. Solve the proportion $\dfrac{7x}{11}=\dfrac{14}{33}$.

A. $x=1$

B. $x=3$

C. $x=\dfrac{2}{3}$

D. $x=\dfrac{3}{2}$

18. The results of Miam's tennis games follow: 7 wins, 3 losses, 5 ties. What is the ratio of her ties to her losses?

A. $\dfrac{3}{5}$

B. $\dfrac{5}{7}$

C. $\dfrac{5}{7}$

D. $\dfrac{5}{3}$

19. Marcus has 12 pennies for every 16 dimes he has. What is the simplified ratio of dimes to pennies that he has?

A. $\dfrac{3}{2}$

B. $\dfrac{1}{1}$

C. $\dfrac{4}{3}$

D. $\dfrac{2}{7}$

20. Express the ratio 56 to 42 as a fraction in simplest form.

A. $\dfrac{8}{7}$

B. $\dfrac{4}{3}$

C. $\dfrac{3}{4}$

D. $\dfrac{7}{8}$

Answers to the Exercises

Exercise 1

1. **6 to 24**

   $$= \frac{6}{24} \quad \text{Divide both numbers by 6 to simplify.} \quad = \frac{1}{4}$$

2. **10 to 62**

   $$= \frac{10}{62} \quad \text{Divide both numbers by 2 to simplify.} \quad = \frac{5}{31}$$

3. **3 yards to 5 feet** **(3 feet = 1 yard)**

   3 yards = 9 feet

   Now write 9 feet to 5 feet as a fraction and cancel "feet."

   $$\frac{9feet}{5feet} = \frac{9}{5}$$

4. $\dfrac{12}{16}$ **Divide both numbers by 2.** $= \dfrac{6}{8}$ **Divide by 2 again.** $= \dfrac{3}{4}$

   $$\frac{3}{4} \quad \text{or} \quad 3 \text{ to } 4 \quad \text{or} \quad 3:4$$

5. $\dfrac{4}{8}$ **Divide both numbers by 2.** $= \dfrac{1}{2}$

6.   3 to 17   or   3:17   or $\dfrac{3}{17}$

   The 3 comes first because the ratio is losses to wins.

7. $3.40 to $2.10

   Multiply by 10 to move the decimal over.

   34 to 21   or $\dfrac{34}{21}$ or   34:21

Exercise 2

1. $\dfrac{2}{5} = \dfrac{14}{z}$

   Cross multiply. $2z = 14(5)$

   Divide by 2. $2z = 70$

                          $z = 35$

2. $\dfrac{2y}{7} = \dfrac{-3}{9}$

   Cross multiply. $9(2y) = -3(7)$

   Divide by 18. $18y = -21$

   Divide both numbers by 3. $y = \dfrac{-21}{18}$

                                    $y = -\dfrac{7}{6}$

3. $\dfrac{-3}{-2} = \dfrac{x+8}{-x+17}$

   Cross multiply and distribute. $-3(-x + 17) = -2(x + 8)$

   Move x's to the left. $3x - 51 = -2x - 16$

   Move 51 to the right by adding. $5x - 51 = -16$

   Divide by 5. $5x = 35$

                                       $x = 7$

4. $\dfrac{4}{5y} = \dfrac{8}{10}$

   Cross multiply. $4(10) = 8(5y)$

   Divide by 40. $40 = 40y$

                         $y = 1$

5. $\dfrac{40}{50} = \dfrac{x}{90}$

   Cross multiply. $40(90) = 50x$

   Divide by 50. $3600 = 50x$

                         $x = 72$

6. $\dfrac{10}{6} = \dfrac{x}{24}$

   Cross multiply. $10(24) = 6x$

   Divide by 6. $240 = 6x$

                         $x = 40$

   If Jodie has 24 shorts, then she has 40 shirts.

Answers to the Chapter Quiz

1. **A**

$$\frac{14}{21} = \frac{2}{3}$$

2. **B**

$$\frac{18}{16} = \frac{9}{8} \quad \text{Be careful of the order!}$$

3. **B**

$$\frac{10}{21} = \frac{2x}{3x-6}$$
$$10(3x-6) = 21(2x)$$
$$30x - 60 = 42x$$
$$-12x = 60$$
$$x = -5$$

4. **D**

Be careful of the order!

5. **C**

$$\frac{\text{pages}}{\text{minutes}} = \frac{20}{50} = \frac{60}{x}$$
$$20x = 50(60) = 3,000$$
$$x = 150$$

6. D

Be careful of the order!

7. B

$$\frac{5 \text{ feet}}{3 \text{ inches}} = \frac{5(12) \text{ inches}}{3 \text{ inches}} = \frac{60}{3} = \frac{20}{1}$$

8. C

$$\frac{\text{pens}}{\text{notebooks}} = \frac{8}{6} = \frac{x}{21}$$
$$6x = 8(21) = 168$$
$$x = 28$$

9. B

$$\frac{15}{42} = \frac{5}{14}$$

10. D

$$\frac{\text{hours}}{\text{minutes}} = \frac{3}{27} = \frac{3(60)}{27} = \frac{180}{27} = \frac{20}{3}$$

11. A

$$\frac{\text{gals}}{\text{guys}} = \frac{6}{7} = \frac{x}{21}$$
$$7x = 6(21) = 126$$
$$x = 18$$

12. D

$$\frac{24}{40} = \frac{3}{5}$$

13. C

$$\frac{\text{inches}}{\text{feet}} = \frac{15}{4} = \frac{15}{4(12)} = \frac{15}{48} = \frac{5}{16}$$

14. C

$$\frac{\text{pages}}{\text{minutes}} = \frac{21}{35} = \frac{x}{20}$$
$$35x = 21(20) = 420$$
$$x = \frac{420}{35} = \frac{60}{5} = 12$$

15. A

$$\frac{\text{nickels}}{\text{dimes}} = \frac{24}{16} = \frac{3}{2}$$

16. D

$$\frac{14}{49} = \frac{2}{7}$$

17. C

$$\frac{7x}{11} = \frac{14}{33}$$

$$33(7x) = 11(14)$$

$$231x = 154$$

$$x = \frac{154}{231} = \frac{22}{33} = \frac{2}{3}$$

18. D

$$\frac{\text{ties}}{\text{losses}} = \frac{5}{3} \quad \text{Be careful of the order!}$$

19. C

$$\frac{\text{dimes}}{\text{pennies}} = \frac{16}{12} = \frac{4}{3} \quad \text{Be careful of the order!}$$

20. B

$$\frac{56}{42} = \frac{8}{6} = \frac{4}{3}$$

Chapter 6
Radical Expressions

This section involves the following skills:

1. You should be able to simplify and perform operations on radical expressions and equations.

2. You should be able to rationalize square root expressions and understand and use the concepts of negative and rational exponents.

3. You should be able to add, subtract, multiply, divide, and simplify radical expressions and expressions with rational exponents.

4. You should be able to solve radical equations and equations with terms that have rational exponents.

The following standards are assessed on the Florida's Algebra 1 End-of-Course exam either directly or indirectly:

MA.912.A.6.1   Simplify radical expressions.

MA.912.A.6.2   Add, subtract, multiply, and divide radical expressions (square roots and higher).

Radical expressions

Radical sign $\sqrt{}$ indicates the square root symbol

Radicand – the value that is under the radical sign

Index number – tells us how many of the same number we need to multiply to get the radicand.

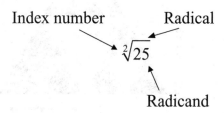

Index number   Radical

$\sqrt[2]{25}$

Radicand

$\sqrt[2]{}$ or $\sqrt{}$ If you do not see the index, it is assumed to be 2. Looking for two of the same number.

$\sqrt[3]{}$ Looking for 3 of the same number.

$\sqrt[4]{}$ Looking for 4 of the same number.

Perfect squares

It is helpful to memorize **perfect squares**: the product of a number with itself. If you memorize the following chart, the process of simplifying radicals becomes both easier and faster.

Numbers	Perfect Square
1•1	1
2•2	4
3•3	9
4•4	16
5•5	25
6•6	36
7•7	49
8•8	64
9•9	81
10•10	100

Simplifying radicals

In order to simplify radicals, you need to remember two important rules:

1. Product Property of square roots

$\sqrt{ab}$ is the same as $\sqrt{a} \bullet \sqrt{b}$ where a and $b > 0 \geq$ zero

2. Division Property of square roots

$\sqrt{\dfrac{a}{b}}$ is the same as $\dfrac{\sqrt{a}}{\sqrt{b}}$ where both a and b are $\geq$ zero

Do you remember those prime factorization trees you learned in elementary school?

$$49 \nearrow\searrow 7 \bullet 7$$

$$= 7 \bullet 7$$

$$36 \nearrow\searrow 6 \bullet 6$$

$$= 6 \bullet 6$$

$$48$$
$$6 \bullet 8$$
$$2 \bullet 3 \quad 2 \bullet 4$$
$$2 \bullet 2$$

$$= 2 \bullet 2 \bullet 2 \bullet 2 \bullet 3$$

$$50$$
$$10 \bullet 5$$
$$2 \bullet 5$$

$$= 2 \bullet 5 \bullet 5$$

Example:

Simplify $\sqrt{40}$.

Factor down to prime numbers.

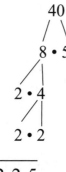

$= \sqrt{2 \; 2 \; 2 \; 5}$

Because the index number is two, you need two of the same number to come out from underneath the radical.

Tip: Think of a pair of numbers like a pair of people going out on a date. They are two people (two numbers under the radical) but they are only <u>one</u> couple (the two numbers come out as one couple/number).

$\sqrt{(2 \; 2) \; 2 \; 5}$

The pair of twos goes out on a date as one couple.

$2\sqrt{2 \cdot 5}$

Because the 2 and 5 do not have a date, they have to stay in the house.

Multiply anything left in the house.

$= 2\sqrt{10}$

Example:

Simplify $\sqrt{60}$.

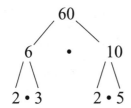

$$\sqrt{(2 \cdot 2) \cdot 3 \cdot 5}$$

$$= 2\sqrt{3 \cdot 5}$$

$$= 2\sqrt{15}$$

Example:

Simplify. $\sqrt{36}$.

(Note: 36 is a perfect square = 6 • 6.)

We have a pair so we can stop.

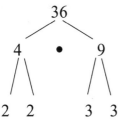

$2 \cdot 3 = 6$ When more than one number comes out of the house, multiply them together.

Example:

Simplify $\sqrt{80}$.

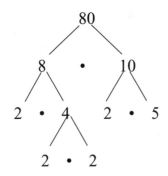

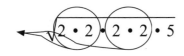

$2 \cdot 2 \sqrt{5}$

$= 4\sqrt{5}$

Example:

Simplify $2\sqrt{8}$.

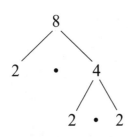

$2\sqrt{2 \cdot 2 \cdot 2}$

When the 2 comes outside, it is multiplied by the number on the outside, 2.

$= 2 \cdot 2 \sqrt{2}$

$= 4\sqrt{2}$

Example:

$3\sqrt{24}$

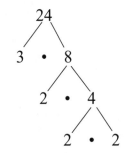

$3\sqrt{2 \cdot 2 \cdot 2 \cdot 3}$

$= 3 \cdot 2 \sqrt{2 \cdot 3}$

$= 6\sqrt{6}$

Example:

Simplify $\sqrt{20a^3}$.

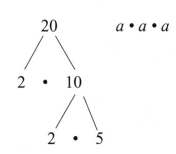

$= \sqrt{2 \cdot 2 \cdot 5 \cdot a \cdot a \cdot a}$

$= 2a\sqrt{5a}$

Example:

Simplify $\sqrt{32x^2y}$.

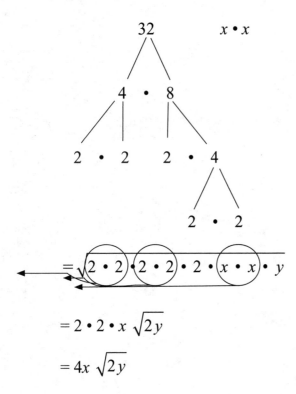

$$= 2 \cdot 2 \cdot x \sqrt{2y}$$

$$= 4x \sqrt{2y}$$

Exercise 1

Complete each of the following questions.

1. **Simplify $\sqrt{8}$.**

2. **Simplify $\sqrt{36}$.**

3. **Simplify $\sqrt{45}$.**

4. **Simplify $\sqrt{\dfrac{4}{25}}$.**

Adding and subtracting square roots

Just like fractions, in order to arrive at the common denominator, you have to have the same value inside the radicand in order to add or subtract square roots (you need *like* radicals).

Example:

$$2\sqrt{5} + 3\sqrt{5} = \underline{\hspace{1cm}}$$

Add the outside numbers (2 and 3).

$$= (2+3)\sqrt{5}$$

Number inside (radicand) stays the same.

$$= 5\sqrt{5}$$

Example:

$$4\sqrt{6} - 3\sqrt{6} = \underline{\hspace{1cm}}$$

Subtract the outside numbers (4 and 3).

$$= (4-3)\sqrt{6}$$

$$= 1\sqrt{6} \text{ or } \sqrt{6}$$

Example:

$$4\sqrt{2} - 2\sqrt{2} = \underline{\hspace{1cm}}$$

Subtract the outside numbers (4 and 2).

$$= (4-2)\sqrt{2}$$

$$= 2\sqrt{2}$$

Example:

$$4\sqrt{7} + 3\sqrt{7} - 2\sqrt{7} + 4\sqrt{2} = \underline{\qquad}$$

Add or subtract outside numbers. Note that they are not all like radicands.

$$= (4 + 3 - 2)\sqrt{7} + 4\sqrt{2}$$

$$= 5\sqrt{7} + 4\sqrt{2}$$

Example:

$$4\sqrt{3} + 2\sqrt{11} - 4\sqrt{11} + 8\sqrt{3} = \underline{\qquad}$$

Add or subtract outside numbers of like radicands.

$$= (4 + 8)\sqrt{3} + (2 - 4)\sqrt{11}$$

$$= 12\sqrt{3} - 2\sqrt{11}$$

Example:

$$3\sqrt{2} + \sqrt{32} = \underline{\qquad}$$

Let's see if we can simplify $\sqrt{32}$ and have a radicand of 2.

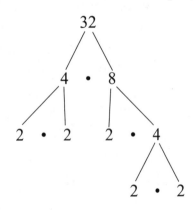

$$= \sqrt{(2 \cdot 2) \cdot (2 \cdot 2) \cdot 2} \quad = 4\sqrt{2}$$

$$= 3\sqrt{2} + 4\sqrt{2}$$

$$= 7\sqrt{2}$$

Example:

$$7\sqrt{12} - 2\sqrt{2} =$$

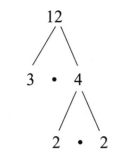

$$= \sqrt{(2 \cdot 2) \cdot 3} = 2\sqrt{3}$$

$$= 7 \cdot 2\sqrt{3} - 2\sqrt{2}$$

$$= 14\sqrt{3} - 2\sqrt{2}$$

You can't combine because these are not like radicals.

Example:

$$3\sqrt{2} + \sqrt{4} - 3\sqrt{8} = \underline{\qquad}$$

Break down 4 and 8.

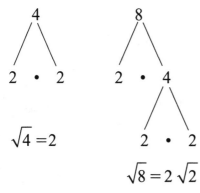

$$\sqrt{4} = 2 \qquad \sqrt{8} = 2\sqrt{2}$$

$$3\sqrt{8} = 3 \cdot 2\sqrt{2}$$

$$3\sqrt{2} + \sqrt{4} - 3\sqrt{8} = 3\sqrt{2} + 2 - 6\sqrt{2}$$

Now, combine like radicands.

$$= -3\sqrt{2} + 2 \quad \text{or} \quad 2 - 3\sqrt{2}$$

Multiplying square roots

When multiplying square roots, first multiply the outside numbers and then multiply the inside numbers. Finally, simplify the square root.

Example:

$$\sqrt{3} \cdot \sqrt{8} \quad = \qquad 1 \cdot 1 \quad \sqrt{3 \cdot 8}$$

Outsides   Insides

$$= 1\sqrt{24} \quad \text{or} \quad \sqrt{24}$$

Now, simplify.

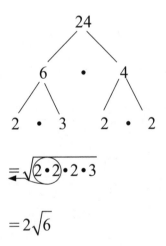

$$= \sqrt{(2 \cdot 2) \cdot 2 \cdot 3}$$

$$= 2\sqrt{6}$$

Example:

$$4\sqrt{20} \cdot -2\sqrt{4} \qquad = \qquad 4 \cdot -2 \qquad \sqrt{20 \cdot 4}$$

$$= -8\sqrt{80}$$

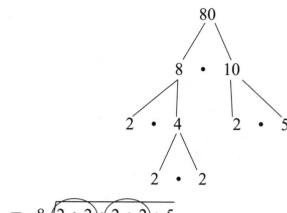

$$=-8\sqrt{2\cdot2\cdot2\cdot2\cdot5}$$

$$=-8\cdot2\cdot2\sqrt{5}$$

$$=-32\sqrt{5}$$

Example:

$$\sqrt{3}\left(2\sqrt{3}+\sqrt{6}\right) \qquad \text{Distribute.}$$

$$=\left(\sqrt{3}\cdot2\sqrt{3}\right)+\left(\sqrt{3}\cdot\sqrt{6}\right)$$

$$=2\sqrt{9}+\sqrt{18} \qquad \text{Now see if you can simplify.}$$

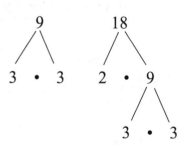

$$=2\cdot3+3\sqrt{2}$$

$$=6+3\sqrt{2}$$

Example:

$$3\sqrt{5}\left(-2\sqrt{2}-3\sqrt{12}\right) \qquad \text{Distribute.}$$

$$=\left(3\sqrt{5}\cdot-2\sqrt{2}\right)-\left(3\sqrt{5}\cdot3\sqrt{12}\right)$$

$$=-6\sqrt{10}-9\sqrt{60} \qquad \text{Now break down radicands.}$$

```
        10              60
       / \             / \
      2 • 5           2 • 30
                          /
                         3 • 10
                            / \
                           2 • 5
```

$$=-6\sqrt{10}-9\cdot2\sqrt{15}$$

$$=-6\sqrt{10}-18\sqrt{15}$$

Example:

$$\left(\sqrt{5}+\sqrt{2}\right)\left(\sqrt{3}+\sqrt{6}\right) \qquad \text{F.O.I.L.} \qquad \text{First, Outer, Inner, Last}$$

$$\qquad\quad \text{F} \qquad\qquad \text{O} \qquad\qquad \text{I} \qquad\qquad \text{L}$$

$$\left(\sqrt{5\cdot3}\right) \qquad \left(\sqrt{5\cdot6}\right) \qquad \left(\sqrt{2\cdot3}\right) \qquad \left(\sqrt{2\cdot6}\right)$$

$$=\sqrt{15}+\sqrt{30}+\sqrt{6}+\sqrt{12} \qquad \text{Break down radicands if possible.}$$

$$=\sqrt{15}+\sqrt{30}+\sqrt{6}+2\sqrt{3}$$

Example:

$$\left(\sqrt{3}+\sqrt{6}\right)\left(2\sqrt{5}+4\sqrt{7}\right) \qquad \text{F.O.I.L.}$$

$$\left(\sqrt{3}\cdot 2\sqrt{5}\right)+\left(\sqrt{3}\cdot 4\sqrt{7}\right)+\left(\sqrt{6}\cdot 2\sqrt{5}\right)+\left(\sqrt{6}\cdot 4\sqrt{7}\right)$$

$$=2\sqrt{15}+4\sqrt{21}+2\sqrt{30}+4\sqrt{42}$$

Simplify if possible. None of these numbers can be broken down; therefore, this is the simplified form.

Example:

$$\left(4+\sqrt{7}\right)^2$$

$$\left(4+\sqrt{7}\right)\left(4+\sqrt{7}\right) \qquad \text{Squared is to multiply it by itself.}$$

$$=16+4\sqrt{7}+4\sqrt{7}+\sqrt{7\cdot 7} \qquad \text{F.O.I.L.}$$

$$=16+8\sqrt{7}+7 \qquad \text{Combine like radicands.}$$

$$23+8\sqrt{7} \qquad \text{Simplified by combining constants.}$$

Dividing radicals

Example:

$$\sqrt{\frac{8}{2}}=\underline{\qquad} \qquad \text{Simplify} \quad \sqrt{4}=2$$

Example:

$$\sqrt{\frac{3}{25}} = \underline{\quad\quad} \quad \text{Rewrite} \quad \frac{\sqrt{3}}{\sqrt{25}} \text{, then simplify} \quad \frac{\sqrt{3}}{5}$$

Example:

$$\frac{5}{\sqrt{3}}$$

Remember that the denominator cannot be a radical so multiply numerator and denominator by $\sqrt{3}$.

$$\frac{5}{\sqrt{3}}\left(\frac{\sqrt{3}}{\sqrt{3}}\right) = \frac{5\sqrt{3}}{\sqrt{9}} = \frac{5\sqrt{3}}{3}$$

Example:

$$\frac{3\sqrt{2}}{\sqrt{6}}$$

$$\frac{3\sqrt{2}}{\sqrt{6}}\left(\frac{\sqrt{6}}{\sqrt{6}}\right) = \frac{3\sqrt{12}}{\sqrt{36}} = \frac{6\sqrt{3}}{6} = \sqrt{3}$$

Example:

$$\frac{5}{\sqrt{2}-\sqrt{3}}$$

Multiply by the conjugate of the denominator (change the sign in the middle).

$$\frac{5}{\sqrt{2}-\sqrt{3}}\left(\frac{\sqrt{2}+\sqrt{3}}{\sqrt{2}+\sqrt{3}}\right)=\frac{5\sqrt{2}+5\sqrt{3}}{\sqrt{4}+\sqrt{6}-\sqrt{6}-\sqrt{9}}=\frac{5\left(\sqrt{2}+\sqrt{3}\right)}{2-3}=\frac{5\left(\sqrt{2}+\sqrt{3}\right)}{-1}$$
$$=-5\left(\sqrt{2}+\sqrt{3}\right)$$

Exercise 2

Complete each of the following questions.

1. Simplify: $5\sqrt{48a}$.

2. Multiply and simplify: $\sqrt{10b^2} \cdot \sqrt{3b}$.

3. Rationalize the denominator (get the radical out of the denominator):

    $$\frac{5}{\sqrt{2}}.$$

4. Multiply and simplify: $\left(\sqrt{2}+5\right)^2$.

5. Multiply and simplify: $\left(5+\sqrt{6}\right)\left(5-\sqrt{6}\right)$.

6. Simplify: $\sqrt{\dfrac{12x^5}{81}}$.

7. Simplify: $\dfrac{5\sqrt{6}}{\sqrt{3n}}$.

8. Perform the indicated operation: $2\sqrt{3} + 4\sqrt{3}$.

9. Perform the indicated operation and simplify: $\sqrt{2} + \sqrt{9} + \sqrt{16}$.

10. Perform the indicated operation and simplify: $\sqrt{28} - 3\sqrt{7} + \sqrt{3}$.

End-of-Chapter Quiz: Radical Expressions and Equations

1. Simplify: $\sqrt{625}$.

A. 20.5

B. 25

C. 312.5

D. 205

2. Simplify: $\sqrt[3]{32,000}$.

A. 1,100

B. $20\sqrt[3]{4}$

C. $100\sqrt[3]{4}$

D. $10\sqrt[3]{32}$

3. Simplify: $4\sqrt{6}+3\sqrt{5}-2\sqrt{6}-\sqrt{5}$.

A. $2\sqrt{6}+2\sqrt{5}$

B. $4\sqrt{6}+4\sqrt{5}$

C. $4\sqrt{1}=4$

D. $7\sqrt{1}-3$

4. **Simplify:** $\sqrt{100}$.

A. 10

B. 25

C. 312.5

D. 10,000

5. **Simplify:** $\sqrt[3]{8x^6 y^{12} z^{16}}$.

A. $2x^3 y^9 z^{13}$

B. $2x^2 y^4 z^5 \sqrt[3]{z}$

C. $5x^3 y^9 z^{13}$

D. $5x^2 y^4 z^5 \sqrt[3]{z}$

6. **Simplify:** $4\sqrt{12} - 7\sqrt{50} + 6\sqrt{18}$.

A. $6\sqrt{14}$

B. -9

C. $8\sqrt{3} + 17\sqrt{2}$

D. $8\sqrt{3} - 17\sqrt{2}$

7. Simplify: $\left(4\sqrt{3}-1\right)\left(2\sqrt{3}+5\right)$.

A. $19+18\sqrt{3}$

B. $29+18\sqrt{3}$

C. $19-18\sqrt{3}$

D. $29-18\sqrt{3}$

8. Simplify: $\sqrt{7}\left(2\sqrt{6}-3\right)$.

A. $2\sqrt{42}-3$

B. $6\sqrt{42}$

C. $-6\sqrt{42}$

D. $2\sqrt{42}-3\sqrt{7}$

9. Simplify: $\sqrt{\dfrac{9}{25}}$.

A. $\dfrac{3}{25}$

B. $\dfrac{7}{23}$

C. $.12$

D. $\dfrac{3}{5}$

10. Simplify: $\left(\sqrt{3}-\sqrt{2}\right)^2$.

A. 1

B. $1-2\sqrt{6}$

C. $5+2\sqrt{6}$

D. $5-2\sqrt{6}$

11. Simplify: $\left(\sqrt{12}\right)\left(\sqrt{6}\right)$.

A. $36\sqrt{2}$

B. 6

C. $6\sqrt{2}$

D. $6\sqrt{6}$

12. Simplify: $\dfrac{6}{\sqrt{3}}$.

A. $\sqrt{2}$

B. $3\sqrt{3}$

C. $2\sqrt{3}$

D. 2

13. Simplify: $\dfrac{12}{2-\sqrt{3}}$.

A. $-2\sqrt{3}$

B. $24-12\sqrt{3}$

C. $2\sqrt{3}$

D. $24+12\sqrt{3}$

14. Perform the indicated operation: $7\sqrt{5}-3\sqrt{5}$.

A. $10\sqrt{5}$

B. 4

C. $4\sqrt{5}$

D. 20

15. Simplify: $\sqrt{3}\cdot\sqrt{27}$.

A. $\sqrt{30}$

B. $6\sqrt{5}$

C. 9

D. 15

16. **Perform the indicated operation and simplify:** $7\sqrt{3}-5\sqrt{10}+6\sqrt{12}$.

   A. $19\sqrt{3}-5\sqrt{10}$

   B. $8\sqrt{5}$

   C. $19\sqrt{3}+5\sqrt{10}$

   D. $13\sqrt{5}-5\sqrt{10}$

17. **Simplify:** $6\sqrt{24a^2}$.

   A. $12a\sqrt{6}$

   B. $12a$

   C. $25a-1$

   D. $8a\sqrt{2}$

18. **Simplify:** $\sqrt{32a^2}\cdot\sqrt{2b}$.

   A. $a\sqrt{34b}$

   B. $16a\sqrt{2b}$

   C. $8a\sqrt{b}$

   D. $8ab$

19. Simplify: $\sqrt{6} \cdot \sqrt{54}$.

A. $\sqrt{30}$

B. $6\sqrt{5}$

C. 9

D. 18

20. Simplify: $\left(7 + 3\sqrt{2}\right)^2$.

A. 671

B. $67 - 42\sqrt{2}$

C. $58\sqrt{2}$

D. $67 + 42\sqrt{2}$

Answers to the Exercises

Exercise 1

1. Break down 8 into $\sqrt{2 \cdot 2 \cdot 2}$

   $= 2\sqrt{2}$

2. Break down 36 into $\sqrt{6 \cdot 6}$

   $= 6$

3. Break down 45 into $\sqrt{3 \cdot 3 \cdot 5}$

   $= 3\sqrt{5}$

4. Rewrite: $\dfrac{\sqrt{4}}{\sqrt{25}} = \dfrac{2}{5}$

Exercise 2

1. Break down 48 into $5\sqrt{2 \cdot 2 \cdot 2 \cdot 2 \cdot 3 \cdot a} = 5 \cdot 2 \cdot 2\sqrt{3a}$

   $= 20\sqrt{3a}$

2. Multiply the 10 and the 3; Multiply the variable by adding the exponents.

   $\sqrt{30b^3} = \sqrt{2 \cdot 3 \cdot 5 \cdot b \cdot b \cdot b} = b\sqrt{30b}$

3. Multiply everything (top and bottom) by $\sqrt{2}$.

$$\frac{5}{\sqrt{2}}\left(\frac{\sqrt{2}}{\sqrt{2}}\right)=\frac{5\sqrt{2}}{\sqrt{4}}=\frac{5\sqrt{2}}{2}$$

4. First, rewrite $(\sqrt{2}+5)(\sqrt{2}+5)$

   F.O.I.L. $\quad \sqrt{4}+5\sqrt{2}+5\sqrt{2}+25$

   Combine like radicands and simplify. $\quad =2+10\sqrt{2}+25$

   $=27+10\sqrt{2}$

5. F.O.I.L. $\quad 25-5\sqrt{6}+5\sqrt{6}-\sqrt{36}$

   Combine like radicals and simplify. $25-6=19$

6. Break down $\sqrt{\dfrac{2\cdot 2\cdot 3\cdot x\cdot x\cdot x\cdot x\cdot x}{9\cdot 9}}=\dfrac{2x^2\sqrt{3x}}{9}$

7. $\dfrac{5\sqrt{6}}{\sqrt{3n}}\left(\dfrac{\sqrt{3n}}{\sqrt{3n}}\right)=\dfrac{5\sqrt{18n}}{\sqrt{9n^2}}=\dfrac{5\cdot 3\sqrt{2n}}{3n}=\dfrac{15\sqrt{2n}}{3n}=\dfrac{5\sqrt{2n}}{n}$

8. $=6\sqrt{3}$

   Add the outside numbers $=(2+4)\sqrt{3}$

9. Break down the 9 into $\sqrt{3\cdot 3}=3$

   and Break down the 16 into $\sqrt{4\cdot 4}=4$

$$\sqrt{2}+3+4$$

$$=7+\sqrt{2}$$

10. Break down 28 into $\sqrt{2 \cdot 2 \cdot 7} = 2\sqrt{7}$.

$$2\sqrt{7}-3\sqrt{7}+\sqrt{3}$$

$$(2-3)\sqrt{7}+\sqrt{3}$$

$$=-\sqrt{7}+\sqrt{3}$$

Answers to the Chapter Quiz

1. **B**

    $$25 \times 25 = 625$$

2. **B**

    $$\sqrt[3]{32,000} = \sqrt[3]{1,000 \times 32} = 10\sqrt[3]{32} = 10\sqrt[3]{8 \times 4} = 10 \times 2\sqrt[3]{4} = 20\sqrt[3]{4}$$

3. **A**

    Combine like terms: $4\sqrt{6}+3\sqrt{5}-2\sqrt{6}-\sqrt{5}=2\sqrt{6}+2\sqrt{5}$

4. **A**

$$10 \times 10 = 100$$

5. **B**

$$\sqrt[3]{8x^6 y^{12} z^{16}} = \sqrt[3]{8}\left(\sqrt[3]{x^6}\right)\left(\sqrt[3]{y^{12}}\right)\left(\sqrt[3]{z^{16}}\right) = 2\left(x^2\right)\left(y^4\right)\left(\sqrt[3]{z^{15}z}\right) = 2x^2 y^4 z^5 \sqrt[3]{z}$$

6. **D**

$$4\sqrt{12} - 7\sqrt{50} + 6\sqrt{18} = 4\sqrt{4\times3} - 7\sqrt{25\times2} + 6\sqrt{9\times2}$$
$$= 4\times2\sqrt{3} - 7\times5\sqrt{2} + 6\times3\sqrt{2} = 8\sqrt{3} - 35\sqrt{2} + 18\sqrt{2} = 8\sqrt{3} - 17\sqrt{2}$$

7. **A**

$$\left(4\sqrt{3} - 1\right)\left(2\sqrt{3} + 5\right) = 4\sqrt{3}\left(2\sqrt{3} + 5\right) - 1\left(2\sqrt{3} + 5\right) = 24 + 20\sqrt{3} - 2\sqrt{3} - 5$$
$$= 19 + 18\sqrt{3}$$

8. **D**

$$\sqrt{7}\left(2\sqrt{6} - 3\right) = 2\sqrt{42} - 3\sqrt{7}$$

9. **D**

$$\sqrt{\frac{9}{25}} = \frac{\sqrt{9}}{\sqrt{25}} = \frac{3}{5}$$

10. D

$$(\sqrt{3}-\sqrt{2})^2 = (\sqrt{3}-\sqrt{2})(\sqrt{3}-\sqrt{2}) = \sqrt{3}(\sqrt{3}-\sqrt{2})-\sqrt{2}(\sqrt{3}-\sqrt{2})$$
$$= 3-\sqrt{6}-\sqrt{6}+2 = 5-2\sqrt{6}$$

11. C

$$\left(\sqrt{12}\right)\left(\sqrt{6}\right) = \sqrt{72} = \sqrt{36\times 2} = \sqrt{36}\times\sqrt{2} = 6\sqrt{2}$$

12. C

Rationalize the denominator: $\dfrac{6}{\sqrt{3}}\times\dfrac{\sqrt{3}}{\sqrt{3}} = \dfrac{6\sqrt{3}}{3} = 2\sqrt{3}$

13. D

Rationalize the denominator, using the conjugate of the denominator:

$$\frac{12}{\left(2-\sqrt{3}\right)}\times\frac{\left(2+\sqrt{3}\right)}{\left(2+\sqrt{3}\right)} = \frac{12\left(2+\sqrt{3}\right)}{4-3} = \frac{12\left(2+\sqrt{3}\right)}{1} = 12\left(2+\sqrt{3}\right) = 24+12\sqrt{3}$$

14. C

Combine these like terms: $7\sqrt{5}-3\sqrt{5} = 4\sqrt{5}$.

15. C

$$\sqrt{3}\bullet\sqrt{27} = \sqrt{81} = 9$$

16. A

$$7\sqrt{3} - 5\sqrt{10} + 6\sqrt{12} = 7\sqrt{3} - 5\sqrt{10} + 6\sqrt{4 \times 3} = 7\sqrt{3} - 5\sqrt{10} + 6 \times 2\sqrt{3}$$
$$= 7\sqrt{3} - 5\sqrt{10} + 12\sqrt{3} = 19\sqrt{3} - 5\sqrt{10}$$

17. A

$$6\sqrt{24a^2} = 6\sqrt{24}\sqrt{a^2} = 6\sqrt{4 \times 6}\ a = 6a\sqrt{4 \times 6} = 6a(2)\sqrt{6} = 12a\sqrt{6}$$

18. C

$$\sqrt{32a^2} \bullet \sqrt{2b} = \sqrt{64a^2b} = \sqrt{64}\sqrt{a^2}\sqrt{b} = 8a\sqrt{b}$$

19. D

$$\sqrt{6} \bullet \sqrt{54} = \sqrt{324} = \sqrt{4 \times 81} = \sqrt{4}\sqrt{81} = 2(9) = 18$$

20. D

$$(7 + 3\sqrt{2})^2 = (7 + 3\sqrt{2})(7 + 3\sqrt{2}) = 7(7 + 3\sqrt{2}) + 3\sqrt{2}(7 + 3\sqrt{2})$$
$$= 49 + 21\sqrt{2} + 21\sqrt{2} + 18 = 67 + 42\sqrt{2}$$

Chapter 7

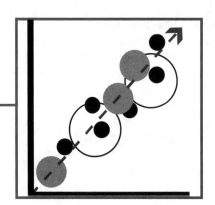

Discrete Mathematics

This section involves the following skills:

1. The test taker should be able to operate with sets, and use set theory to solve problems.

The following standards are assessed on the Florida's Algebra 1 End-of-Course exam either directly or indirectly:

MA.912.D.7.1   Perform set operations such as unions and intersections, complement, and cross product.

MA.912.D.7.2   Use Venn diagrams to explore relationships and patterns and to make arguments about relationships between sets.

Set Theory

A collection of distinct objects is called a **set**. The objects within a set are called **elements**.

Example:

   {5,6,7,8,9}   The elements of the set are 5,6,7,8,9. The symbol to identify a set is brackets "{ }".

Example:

Set J = {2,4,6,8}   To say that 6 is an element of set J, you would write 6 ∈ J.

To say 3 is not an element of set J, you would write 3 ∉ J.

Example:

Given P = {1,3,5,7,9} state whether the following are true or false.

a) 9 ∈ P   b) 7 ∈ P   c) 2 ∈ P   d) 3 ∈ P   e) 0 ∈ P

a) true   b) true   c) false   d) true   e) false

Empty set

An **empty set** is a set with no elements. The symbols for empty set are ∅ or { } Be careful not to confuse the number zero with the empty set.

Subset and universal set

A **Subset** is a smaller part of the universal set.

A **Universal Set** (U) contains all of the elements from which other sets are created.

U= {0,1,2,3,4,5,6,7,8,9} (Universal Set)

V= {1,5,9} (Subset of U)

The symbol for subset is ⊆

Thus, we can write $V \subseteq U$.

Complement

A **complement** of a set is written as V′ or ~V. This is the set of all elements of the universal set not found in set V.

~V = {0,2,3,4,6,7,8} (all elements of U that are not in V.)

Exercise 1

Complete each of the following questions.

U = Universal Set = {1, 2, 3, 4, 5, 6, 7, 8}

Questions 1 − 3 refer to the following.

Given: R = {2,3,4} S = {3,4,5,6,7}   and T = {1,2,3,4,5,6,7}

Find the following:

1. not T

2. not R

3. not S

Questions 4 − 7 refer to the following.

Given: A = {8,9,10,11,12}

Label the following true or false:

4. $5 \in A$

5. $8 \in A$

6. $10 \notin A$

7. $0 \notin A$

Venn Diagram

Venn Diagrams are graphics that show the relationships among sets.

The **union** of sets A and B, written $A \cup B$, is the set of elements, which are in A **or** in B or in both *A* and *B*.

Example:

$A = \{1,2,3,4\}$
$B = \{5,6,7,8\}$
$A \cup B \{1,2,3,4,5,6,7,8\}$

Example:

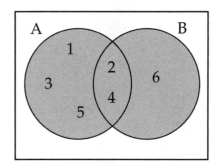

Set A = $\{1,2,3,4,5\}$
Set B = $\{2,4,6\}$
$A \cup B = \{1,2,3,4,5,6\}$

Intersection

The **intersection** of sets A and B, written $A \cap B$, is the set of elements of A that are also elements of B.

Example:

Set J = {1,3,5,7}
Set K = {1,2,3,4,5,6}
$J \cap K$ = {1,3,5}

Example:

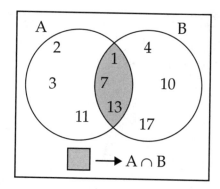

Set A = {1,2,3,7,11,13}
Set B = {1,4,7,10,13,17}
$A \cap B$ = {1,7,13}

If A and B are two sets, the cross product of A and B, written as A × B, is the set of all ordered pairs (x,y) where x is an element of set A and y is an element of set B.

Example:

$A = \{1,2\}$ $B = \{d,e,f\}$

$A \times B = \{(1,d), (1,e), (1,f), (2,d), (2,e), (2,f)\}$

Example:

$A = \{1,2,3\}$ $B = \{4,5\}$

1. $A \times B = \{(1,4), (1,5), (2,4),(2,5), (3,4), (3,5)\}$

2. $B \times A = \{(4,1), (4,2),(4,3), (5,1), (5,2), (5,3)\}$

Exercise 2

Questions 1−3 refer to the following.

Given: $G = \{p,r\}$ $D = \{1,2,3\}$ and $S = \{s,t,u\}$

1. $G \times D =$ _____

2. $D \times S =$ _____

3. $D \times G =$ _____

Questions 4−6 refer to the following.

Given: $A = \{a,b,c\}$ $B = \{c,d,e\}$ and $C = \{e,f\}$

4. $A \cap B$

5. $B \cap C$

6. $C \cup B$

For questions 7—9 use the following Venn Diagram.

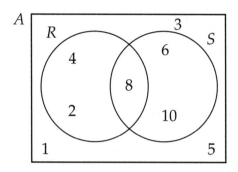

7. $R \cap S$

8. $A \cap S$

9. $R \cup S$

End-of-Chapter Quiz: Set Theory

1. **Set R = {a, b, c, f, g, k} and Set V = {a, d, f, h}. What set represents the intersection of these two sets?**

    A. {a, b, c, d, f, g, h, k}

    B. {a, b, d, h, l}

    C. {a, v}

    D. {a, f}

2. **Which of the following is true, based upon this Venn diagram?**

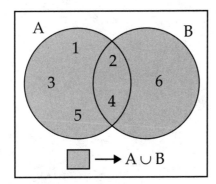

    A. A ∪ B = {1,3,5,6}

    B. A = {1,3,5}

    C. B = {2,4}

    D. A ∩ B = {2,4}

3. **Which set is the complement of A?**

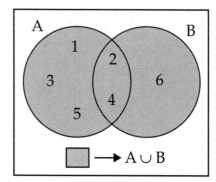

A. $\{1, 3, 5\}$

B. $\{2, 4\}$

C. $\{1, 2, 3, 4, 5\}$

D. $\{6\}$

4. **Set A = {1, 5, 8, 10} and Set B = {a, e, u}. What is A × B?**

A. $\{1, 5, 8, 10, a, e, u\}$

B. $\{(1, a), (1, e), (1, u), (5, a), (5, e), (5, u), (8, a), (8, e), (8, u), (10, a), (10, e),$
    $(10, u)\}$

C. $\{\ \}$

D. $\{(1, a), (5, a), (8, a), (10, a)\}$

5. Given A = {4, 7, 9, 11} and B = {6, 7, 10, 11}, what is A ∪ B?

    A. $\{4, 6\}$

    B. $\{7, 11\}$

    C. $\{4, 6, 9, 10\}$

    D. $\{4, 6, 7, 9, 10, 11\}$

6. Given A = {4, 7, 9, 11} and B = {6, 7, 10, 11}, what is A ∩ B?

    A. $\{4, 6\}$

    B. $\{7, 11\}$

    C. $\{4, 6, 9, 10\}$

    D. $\{4, 6, 7, 9, 10, 11\}$

7. Given A = {4, 9, 11} and B = {6, 7, 10, 11}, which of the following is in A × B?

    A. $(4, 7)$

    B. $(4, 9)$

    C. $(7, 4)$

    D. $(11, 9)$

8. Which of the following is true, given A = {4, 7, 9, 11} and B = {6, 7, 10, 11}?

    A. $4 \in B$

    B. $4 \notin A$

    C. $11 \in B$

    D. $7 \notin B$

9. **If 2 ∈ A and 9 ∈ B, which of the following is true?**

A. $(2, 2) \in A \times B$

B. $A = \{2, 9\}$

C. $B = \{2, 15\}$

D. $(2, 9) \in A \times B$

10. **Given U = {1, 3, 5, 7, 9} and B = {5, 7}, what is the complement of B?**

A. $\{1, 3, 5, 7, 9\}$

B. $\{1, 3\}$

C. $\{1, 3, 9\}$

D. $\{\ \}$

11. **If A = {2, 4, 6} and the complement of A is {5, 7, 10}, what is U?**

A. $\{2, 5\}$

B. $\{\ \}$

C. $\{1, 3, 5\}$

D. $\{2, 4, 5, 6, 7, 10\}$

12 − 16. Use the Venn Diagram.

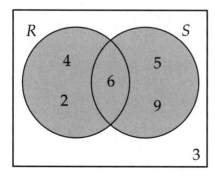

12. What is U?

A.   {2, 3, 4, 6}

B.   {2, 3, 4, 5, 6, 9}

C.   { }

D.   {6}

13. What is R ∩ S?

A.   {2, 3, 4, 6}

B.   {2, 3, 4, 5, 6, 9}

C.   { }

D.   {6}

14. What is the complement of R?

A.   {3, 5, 9}

B.   {2, 3, 4, 5, 6, 9}

C.   { }

D.   {6}

15. What is R ∪ S?

A.   {3, 5, 9}

B.   {2, 4, 5, 6, 9}

C.   { }

D.   {6}

16. What is the complement of S?

A. {3, 5, 9}

B. {2, 3, 4}

C. { }

D. {6}

17. Set P = {2, 10} and Set B = {e, y}. What is P × B?

A. {2, e, 10, y}

B. {(2, e), {(10, y)}

C. {(2, e), (2, y), (10, e), (10, y)}

D. {(e, 2), (y, 10)

18. Set R = {b, d, e, g} and Set Q = {a, b, h}. What set represents the union of these two sets?

A. {a, b, d, e, g, h}

B. {b}

C. { }

D. {a, b, h}

19. Set R = {b, d, e, g} and Set Q = {a, b, h}. What set represents the intersection of these two sets?

A.   {a, b, d, e, g, h}

B.   {b}

C.   { }

D.   {a, b, h}

20. If U = {1, 2, 3, 4, 5, 6, 7}, what is the complement of set A = {1, 3, 5, 7}?

A.   { }

B.   {1, 2, 3}

C.   {2, 4, 6}

D.   {1, 3, 5, 7}

Answers to the Exercises

Exercise 1

1. Looking for numbers that are not found in *T*.

    {8}

2. Looking for numbers that are not found in *R*.

    {1,5,6,7,8}

3. Looking for numbers not found in S.

    {1,2,8}

4. Is 5 included in the set of *A*? No; therefore, this is false.

5. Is 8 included in the set of *A*? Yes; therefore, this is true.

6. Is 10 included in the set of *A*? Yes; therefore, this is false.

7. Is 0 included in the set of *A*? No; therefore, this is true.

Exercise 2

1. Everything in *G* has to be paired with everything in *D*.

    $$= \begin{cases} (p,1), (p,2), (p,3) \\ (r,1),\ (r,2),\ (r,3) \end{cases}$$

2. Everything in *D* has to be paired with everything in *S*.

    $$= \begin{cases} (1,s), (1,t), (1,u) \\ (2,s), (2,t), (2,u) \\ (3,s), (3,t), (3,u) \end{cases}$$

3. Everything in *D* has to be paired with everything in *G*.

    $$= \begin{cases} (1,p), (2,p), (3,p) \\ (1,r), (2,r), (3,r) \end{cases}$$

4. Looking for variables found in *A* and *B*.

    = {c}

5. Looking for variables found in *B* and *C*.

    = {e}

6. Looking for variables found in *C* or *B*.

    = {c,d,e,f}

7. Looking for numbers in *R* and *S* (in the middle where the circles overlap).

   = {8}

8. Looking for numbers in *A* and *S* (anything included in *S*).

   = {6,8,10}

9. Looking for numbers in *R* or *S* (anything in either circle).

   = {2,4,6,8,10}

Answers to the Chapter Quiz

1. **D**

   The intersection includes the elements in both sets.

2. **D**

   That symbol between A and B in choice D means intersection. Hence, choice D states that the elements in both sets are 2 and 4. This is true. Choice A is incorrect because that symbol $\cup$ means union, which is {1, 2, 3, 4, 5, 6}. Choice B is incorrect because A includes 1, 2, 3, 4, and 5. Choice C is incorrect because B includes 2, 4, and 6.

3. **D**

   The complement is the elements in the universe not in the given set.

4. **B**

A × B requires every element of A matched with every element in B. These points make the set A × B.

Since 4 × 3 = 12, there should be 12 points in A × B. The 4 and 3 are the number of elements in A and B, respectively.

5. **D**

A ∪ B requires all of the elements in either A or B or both.

6. **B**

A ∩ B requires all of the elements present in both A and B.

7. **A**

A × B requires every element of A matched with every element in B. These points make the set A × B.

The only choice that has its first element from set A and its second element from set B is choice A.

8. **C**

Choice A states that 4 is an element of B, which is false. Choice B states that 4 is not an element of A, which is false. Choice C is correct because it states that 11 is an element of B, which is true. Choice D is incorrect because it states that 7 is not an element of B, which is false.

9. **D**

A × B requires every element of A matched with every element in B. These points make the set A × B. So, 2 from A would be the first coordinate in a point in A × B and 9 would be the second element in a point in A × B. Thus, the point (2,9) is an element of A × B. Thus, choice D is correct.

10. C

The complement is the elements in the universe not in the given set.

11. D

The complement is the elements in the universe not in the given set. So, U would be all of the elements in A and its complement.

12. B

U is all of the elements in each set, their union, and any elements in the rectangle, but outside the circles.

13. D

This symbol indicates intersection, which means the elements present in both sets. Only 6 is present in both sets.

14. A

The complement is the elements in the universe not in the given set. Be sure to include the 3.

15. B

This symbol indicates union, which means all of the elements in either set, including the intersection of the 2 sets.

16. B

The complement is the elements in the universe not in the given set. Be sure to include the 3.

17. C

P $\times$ B requires every element of P matched with every element in B. These points make the set P $\times$ B. Since 2 $\times$ 2 = 4, there should be 4 points in P $\times$ B. The 2 and 2 are the number of elements in P and B.

18. A

The union of 2 sets is all of the elements in either set, including those in the intersection of the 2 sets.

19. B

The intersection of 2 sets is all of the elements present in both sets.

20. C

The complement is the elements in the universe not in the given set.

Chapter 8

Geometry

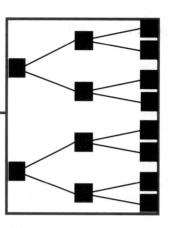

The section involves the following skills:

1. You should be able to understand geometric concepts, applications, and their representations with coordinate systems.

2. You should be able to find lengths and midpoints of line segments, slopes, parallel and perpendicular lines, and equations of lines.

3. You should be able to use a compass and straightedge to construct lines and angles, explaining and justifying the processes used.

4. You should be able to identify types of angles, including those in polygons and those formed by parallel lines cut by a transversal.

5. You should be able to determine perimeters, areas, and angle measures of triangles, squares, and rectangles.

6. You should be able to correctly apply the Pythagorean theorem.

7. You should be able to identify parts of a circle.

The following standards are assessed on the Florida's Algebra 1 End of Course exam either directly or indirectly:

MA.912.G.1.4   Use coordinate geometry to find slopes, parallel lines, perpendicular lines, and equations of lines.

Points, Lines, Angles, and Planes

Angles

Acute angles measure less that 90°. A right angle measures 90°. Obtuse angles measure more than 90° but less than 180°.

Complementary angles total 90°, while supplementary angles total 180°.

Line Segment Lengths

The length of a line segment is determined by using the x and y values of the point (x_1, y_1) and (x_2, y_2). The formula is $d = \sqrt{(x_2 - x_1)^2 + (y_2 - y_1)^2}$. Using the points $(8, -2)$ and $(-6, 0)$, the length of the segment connecting the 2 points is

$$d = \sqrt{(-6 - 8)^2 + (0 - (-2))^2} = \sqrt{(-14)^2 + 2^2} = \sqrt{196 + 4}$$

$$= \sqrt{200} = \sqrt{100 \cdot 2} = \sqrt{100} \cdot \sqrt{2} = 10\sqrt{2}.$$

Line Segment Midpoints

Line segments have midpoints. The midpoint of a segment connecting 2 points is found by averaging the x values of each point and averaging the y values of each point. If a line segment is created connecting points $(8, -2)$ and $(-6, 0)$, the midpoint is $\left(\dfrac{8 + (-6)}{2}, \dfrac{-2 + 0}{2} \right) = \left(\dfrac{2}{2}, \dfrac{-2}{2} \right) = (1, -1)$.

Slope

The **slope** of a line is the ratio of the change in the y-axis coordinates to the change in the x-axis coordinates.

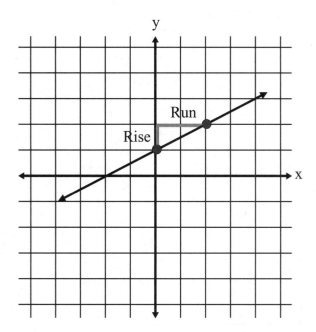

$$\text{Slope } m = \frac{Rise}{Run} \text{ or } \frac{y_2 - y_1}{x_2 - x_1}$$

Ways to Calculate Slope

When given two points, do the following:

Example:

(3,1) and (2,5)

Label the points. $\qquad$ (3,1) and (2,5)

$$(x_1, y_1) \text{ and } (x_2, y_2)$$

Formula $\qquad$ $m = \dfrac{y_2 - y_1}{x_2 - x_1}$

Plug in numbers.	$m = \dfrac{5-1}{2-3}$
Simplify.	$m = \dfrac{4}{-1}$
	$m = -4 \text{ or } \dfrac{-4}{1} \text{ or } \dfrac{4}{-1}$

Example:

(9,–10) and (4,4)

Label the points.	(9,–10) and (4,4)
	(x_1, y_1) and (x_2, y_2)
Formula	$m = \dfrac{y_2 - y_1}{x_2 - x_1}$
Plug in numbers.	$m = \dfrac{4 - (-10)}{4 - 9}$
Simplify.	$m = \dfrac{14}{-5}$
	$m = \dfrac{-14}{5} \text{ or } \dfrac{14}{-5}$

Example:

(–6,–5) and (–4,–9)

Label the points (–6,–5) and (–4,–9).

(x_1, y_1) and (x_2, y_2)

Formula	$m = \dfrac{y_2 - y_1}{x_2 - x_1}$

Plug in numbers.	$m = \dfrac{-9-(-5)}{-4-(-6)}$
Simplify.	$m = \dfrac{-4}{2}$
	$m = -2 \text{ or } \dfrac{-2}{1} \text{ or } \dfrac{2}{-1}$

Example:

(3,2) and (8,2)

Label the points.	(3,2) and (8,2)
	(x_1,y_1) and (x_2,y_2)
Formula	$m = \dfrac{y_2-y_1}{x_2-x_1}$
Plug in numbers.	$m = \dfrac{2-2}{8-3}$
Simplify.	$m = \dfrac{0}{5}$
	$m = 0 \qquad$ (Note: Zero on top only $= 0$)

Example:

(5,3) and (5,–1)

Label the points.	(5,3) and (5,–1)
	(x_1,y_1) and (x_2,y_2)
Formula	$m = \dfrac{y_2-y_1}{x_2-x_1}$
Plug in numbers.	$m = \dfrac{-1-3}{5-5}$

Simplify. $$m = \frac{-4}{0}$$

$m = undefined$

*Zero on the bottom only = undefined

(if zero is <u>UNDER</u> it is <u>undefined</u>)

Remember HOY and VUX.

H-Horizontal line

0-Zero slope

$y=\#$

Horizontal lines have a zero slope and their equations are y equals a number.

V-Vertical line

U-Undefined slope

$x=\#$

Vertical lines have an undefined slope and their equations are x equals a number.

Exercise 1

Find the slope of the line passing through the following:

1. **(0,4) and (–1,2)**

A. $\dfrac{1}{2}$

B. –2

C. 2

D. $-\dfrac{1}{2}$

2. **(–2,5) and (1,–7)**

A. –4

B. 12

C. $-\dfrac{2}{3}$

D. $\dfrac{1}{4}$

3. **(2, –3) and (2,0)**

A. –3

B. 3

C. zero

D. undefined

4. **(1,–6) and (5,–6)**

A. –3

B. 4

C. zero

D. undefined

Finding the slope when given a graph:

Example:

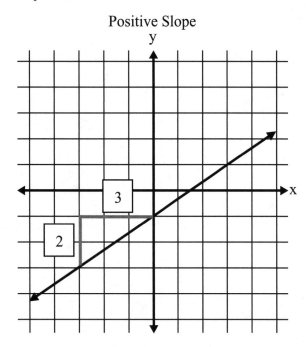

Positive Slope

$$m = \frac{Rise}{Run} = \frac{2}{3} \qquad y\text{-intercept: } (0,-1)$$

Equation of the line graphed: $y = \frac{2}{3}x - 1$

Example:

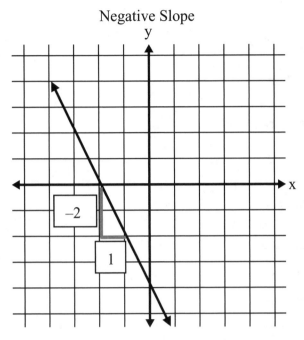

Negative Slope

$$m = \frac{Rise}{Run} = \frac{-2}{1} = -2 \qquad y\text{-intercept: } (0, -4)$$

Equation of the line graphed: $y = -2x - 4$

Example:

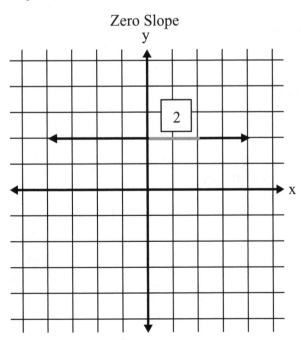

Zero Slope

$$m = \frac{Rise}{Run} = \frac{0}{2} = 0 \qquad \textit{y}\text{-intercept: } (0, 2)$$

Equation of the line graphed: $y = 0x + 2$

$$y = 2$$

*Remember HOY: Horizontal, zero slope, $y = \#$

Example:

Undefined Slope

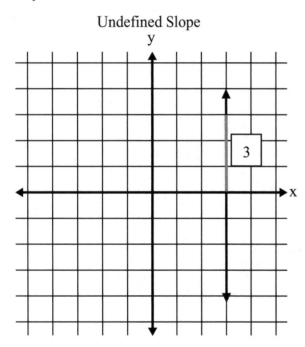

$$m = \frac{Rise}{Run} = \frac{3}{0} = \text{Undefined} \qquad \textit{y}\text{-intercept: n/a}$$

Equation of the line graphed: $x = 3$

*Remember VUX: Vertical line, undefined slope, $x = \#$

Parallel lines

Parallel lines are lines that have the <u>same slope</u>. They run side by side each other and never touch (just like the "l's" in the word parallel).

Example:

Given the equation of a line $y = 2x + 3$, find the equation of a line parallel to it with y-intercept -1.

The slope given is 2; therefore, any line parallel to the given line also has slope 2.

Graph

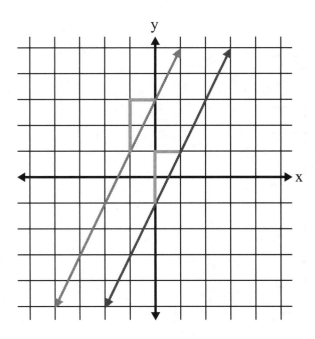

$y = \textcircled{2}x + 3$ and $y = \textcircled{2}x - 1$

Perpendicular lines

Perpendicular lines are lines that have negative reciprocal slopes (opposite sign AND flip the fraction!).

Example:

Given the equation of a line $y = \dfrac{3}{4}x - 2$, find the equation of a line perpendicular to it at its y-intercept.

The slope given is $\dfrac{3}{4}$; therefore, the slope of the perpendicular line is $-\dfrac{4}{3}$.

Graph

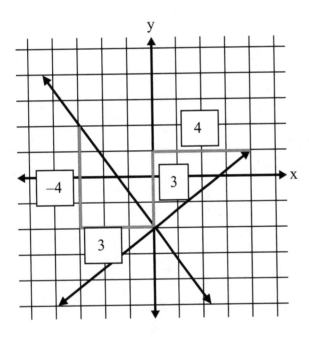

$$y = \left(\dfrac{3}{4}\right)x - 2 \quad \text{and} \quad y = \left(-\dfrac{4}{3}\right)x - 2$$

Exercise 2

Find the slope of the following graphs:

1.

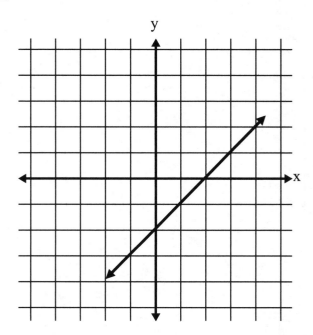

2.

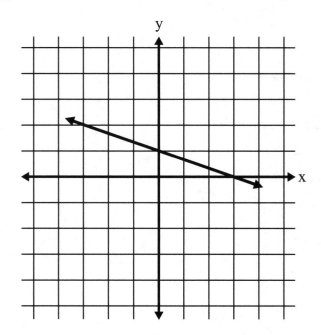

3.

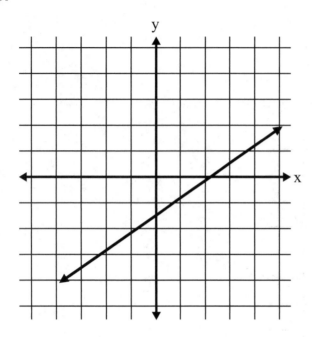

4.

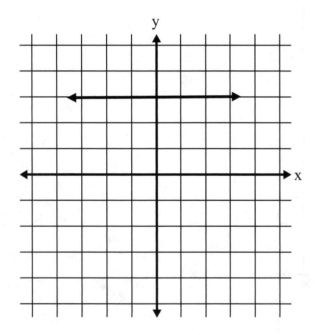

5.

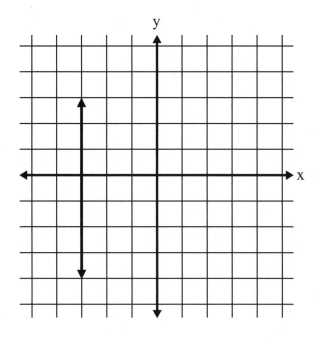

6.

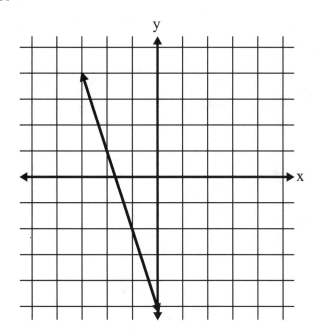

7.   What is the slope of a line parallel to the given line below?

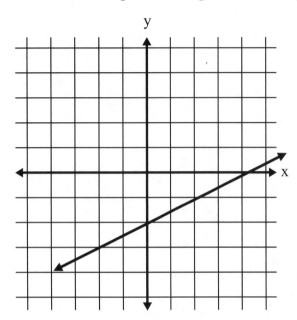

8.   What is the slope of a line perpendicular to the given line below?

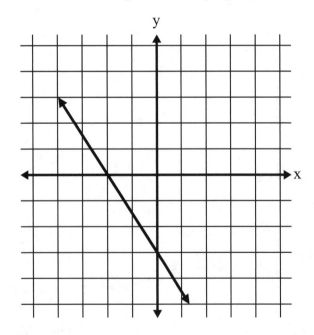

9.   Given the line $y = -\dfrac{1}{3}x + 5$, what would be the slope of a parallel line?

10. Given the line $y = -4x - 3$, what would be the slope of a perpendicular line?

Angles formed by parallel lines cut by a transversal

Parallel lines cut by a transversal typically form two sizes of angles. (The exception to this is if the transversal is perpendicular to the parallel lines. In that case, only right angles are formed.) In the case in which two sized angles are formed, all of the acute angles formed are congruent and all of the obtuse angles formed are congruent. Angles in the same position relative to the parallel lines and the transversal are corresponding angles, such as *A* and *B* below in the diagram. Angles *B* and *C* are alternate interior angles because they are on opposite sides of the transversal and between the 2 parallel lines. Angles *A* and *D* are alternate exterior angles because they are on opposite sides of the transversal and outside the 2 parallel lines. Angles *A* and *C* are vertical angles, since they are across from each other. Vertical angles are always congruent.

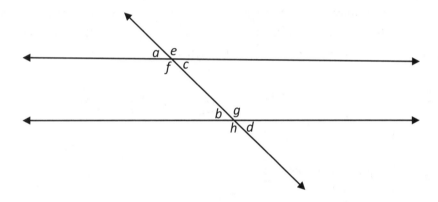

If angle *a* measures 50°, then angles *b, c,* and *d* also measure 50°. The other angles, (*e, f, g,* and *h*), all measure 130°. This is true because any angle *e, f, g, or h* in combination with *a, b, c,* or *d* create a straight line, which equals 180°. (A straight line is also called a straight angle.)

Polygon angle measures

Any triangle's interior angle measures total 180°. The total degrees in the interior angles of any convex quadrilateral, a polygon with four sides, is 360°. (There are also 360° in a circle.)

Any convex polygon has a sum of degrees of its interior angles of 180 times (the number of sides of the polygon – 2). If the polygon is regular, having all equal sides and all equal angles, then each angle of the polygon is 180(the number of sides of the polygon – 2)/(the number of sides of the polygon). By the way, the sum of the measures of all exterior angles of a convex polygon is 360°.

Polygon perimeters and areas

The perimeter of a polygon is found by adding the measures of all of the sides.

The area of a rectangle is found by multiplying the base times the height. The area of a square is found by doing that; however, the base and the height of a square have the same measure. So, the area of a square is the length of the side squared. What about the area of a triangle? The area of a triangle is ½ times the base times the height. Remember that the base and the height must be perpendicular. So, the base of the triangle may need to be extended in order to drop a perpendicular to it to create a height that is perpendicular to the base. (See the following diagram.)

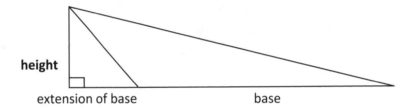

Pythagorean theorem

The Pythagorean theorem is the relationship among the 2 sides and the hypotenuse of any right triangle. If the sides are *a* and *b* and the hypotenuse is *c*, the Pythagorean theorem relationship is $a^2 + b^2 = c^2$.

Let's say a right triangle has a hypotenuse that measures 26 dm and a side that measures 10 dm. The length of the missing side is found as follows:

$$a^2 + b^2 = c^2$$
$$10^2 + b^2 = 26^2$$
$$100 + b^2 = 676$$
$$b^2 = 576$$
$$b = 24.$$

Since *b* is a length of a side of the triangle, that side measures 24 dm.

Circle properties

A circle's radii are all congruent. The radii connect the center of the circle with a point on the circle. A diameter of a circle goes through the center and touches the circle twice. A diameter is twice as long as any radius in the circle. A diameter is the longest chord of a circle. A chord simply extends from one point on the circle to another point on the circle. A portion of the circle is called an arc. The length of an arc is a fraction of the circle's circumference.

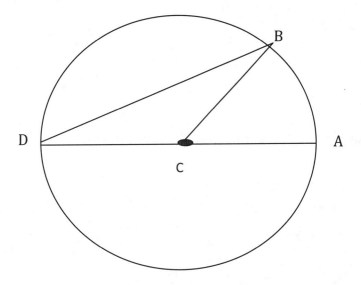

Segment CA is a radius of circle C with center at C. Angle BCA is a central angle because its vertex is at the center of the circle. If the radius of this circle is 10 cm, the circumference of the circle is 20π cm, since the circumference is π times the diameter. The arc that connects A and B, moving counterclockwise from A to B is found by calculating a fraction of the circumference. If the central angle ACB measures 50°, the arc from A to B is $\dfrac{50°}{360°}$ or $\dfrac{5}{36}$ of the entire circumference: $\dfrac{5}{36}$ of 20π cm. That gives an arc measure of $\dfrac{25}{9}\pi$ cm.

Angle ADB is an interior angle, since its vertex is on the circle. By the way, the measure of inscribed angle ADB measures ½ of its intercepted arc. So, if angle ACB measures 50°, angle ADB measures 25°.

End-of-Chapter Quiz: Geometry: Point, Lines, Angles, and Planes

1. What is the complement of a 40° angle?

   A. 50°

   B. 40°

   C. 100°

   D. 130°

2. What is the midpoint of the segment connecting (−3,6) and (5,−2)?

   A. (2,4)

   B. (−1,4)

   C. (1,2)

   D. (−8,6)

3. What is the diagonal of a square with each side measuring $5\sqrt{2}$ ft?

   A. 7 ft

   B. 10 ft

   C. 20 ft

   D. 50 ft

4. What is the supplement of a 60° angle?

A. 20°

B. 30°

C. 100°

D. 120°

5. What is the perimeter of a regular pentagon with each side measuring 10 m?

A. 15 m

B. 40 m

C. 50 m

D. 60 m

6. How many degrees are in the remaining angle of a triangle with angles measuring 20° and 50°?

A. 20

B. 30

C. 100

D. 110

7. If the area of a square is 49 sq cm, what is its perimeter?

A. 196 cm

B. 14 cm

C. 7 cm

D. 28 cm

8. What is the supplement of a 40° angle?

A. 50°

B. 40°

C. 100°

D. 140°

9. Two angles form a straight line. One of the angles measures 9° more than twice the other angle. How many degrees are in the bigger of the 2 angles?

A. 57

B. 114

C. 123

D. 124

10. **What is the perimeter of a square with a side measuring 5 inches?**

   A. 10 inches

   B. 25 square inches

   C. 20 inches

   D. 20 square inches

11. **What is the area of a rectangle with a width of 10 cm and a length of 7 cm?**

   A. 17 cm

   B. 34 cm

   C. 49 sq cm

   D. 70 sq cm

12. **What is the sum of the measures, in degrees, of the interior angles of any rectangle?**

   A. 180

   B. 360

   C. 720

   D. 800

13. What is the midpoint of the segment connecting the origin to the point (−8, 6)?

   A. (3,–4)

   B. (–3,4)

   C. (–4,3)

   D. (4,–3)

14. How many degrees are in one of the acute angles of an isosceles right triangle?

   A. 20

   B. 30

   C. 45

   D. 90

15. How many degrees are in the supplement of an 85° angle?

   A. 5

   B. 10

   C. 15

   D. 95

16. **What is the name of the straight-line segment going through the center of a circle and touching the circle twice?**

   A. an arc

   B. a diameter

   C. a radius

   D. a semi-circle

17. **What is the length of the diagonal of a rectangle with a length of 12 dm and a width of 9 dm?**

   A. 3 dm

   B. 21 dm

   C. 15 dm

   D. 20 dm

18. **If the perimeter of a rectangle is 20 dm and its width is 2 dm, what is its length?**

   A. 18 dm

   B. 22 dm

   C. 2 dm

   D. 8 dm

19. If the area of a square is 144 sq in, what is its perimeter?

A. 12 in

B. 24 in

C. 48 in

D. 576 in

20. How many degrees are in the other acute angle of a right triangle with 1 acute angle measuring 73°?

A. 17

B. 90

C. 107

D. 180

Answers to the Exercises

Exercise 1

1. **C**

$$m = \frac{y_2 - y_1}{x_2 - x_1} = \frac{2-4}{-1-0} = \frac{-2}{-1} = 2$$

2. **A**

$$m = \frac{y_2 - y_1}{x_2 - x_1} = \frac{-7-5}{1-(-2)} = \frac{-12}{3} = -4$$

3. **D**

$$m = \frac{y_2 - y_1}{x_2 - x_1} = \frac{0-(-3)}{2-2} = \frac{3}{0} = \text{undefined}$$

4. **C**

$$m = \frac{y_2 - y_1}{x_2 - x_1} = \frac{-6-(-6)}{5-1} = \frac{0}{4} = \text{zero}$$

Exercise 2

1.

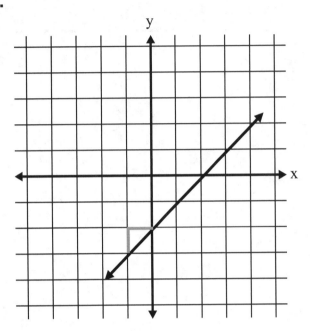

$$m = \frac{Rise}{Run} = \frac{1}{1} = 1$$

2.

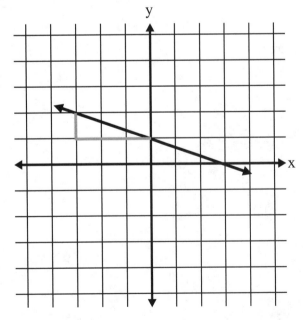

$$m = \frac{Rise}{Run} = \frac{-1}{3}$$

3.

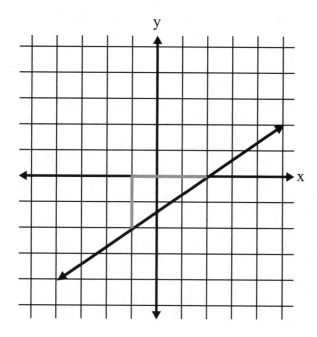

$$m = \frac{Rise}{Run} = \frac{2}{3}$$

4.

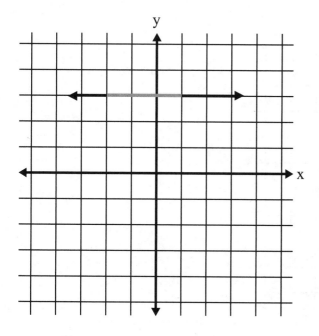

$$m = \frac{Rise}{Run} = \frac{0}{3} = zero$$

5.

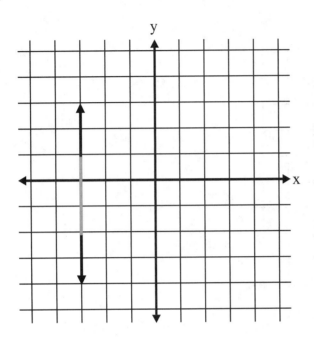

$$m = \frac{Rise}{Run} = \frac{3}{0} = \text{undefined}$$

6.

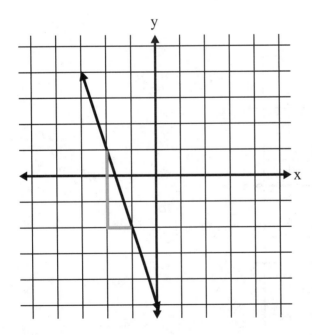

$$m = \frac{Rise}{Run} = \frac{-3}{1} = -3$$

7.

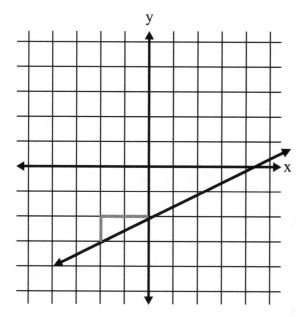

$$m = \frac{Rise}{Run} = \frac{1}{2}$$

8.

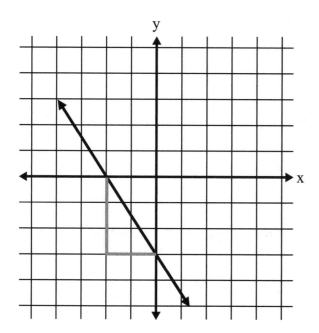

$m = \dfrac{Rise}{Run}$. **The slope of this line is** $\dfrac{-3}{2}$. **Perpendicular lines have negative reciprocal slopes. So, the slope of a line perpendicular to this line is** $\dfrac{2}{3}$.

9. $m = -\dfrac{1}{3}$

   Parallel lines have the SAME slope

10. $m = \dfrac{1}{4}$

    Perpendicular lines have the NEGATIVE RECIPROCAL slope

    (Change the sign, flip the fraction.)

Answers to the Chapter Quiz

1. **A**

   The sum of complementary angles is 90°.

2. **C**

   Average the x's and average the y's to create the midpoint.

3. **B**

   Use the Pythagorean Theorem: $\text{leg}_1^2 + \text{leg}_2^2 = h^2$, where h is the length of the hypotenuse.

   $\left(5\sqrt{2}\right)^2 + \left(5\sqrt{2}\right)^2 = c^2$. Thus, $50 + 50 = c^2$, which is $100 = c^2$, making $c = 10$.

4. **D**

   The sum of supplementary angles is 180°.

5. C

A pentagon has 5 sides. The perimeter of a polygon is the sum of the lengths of all sides. Hence, 5 times 10 m is 50 m.

6. D

The sum of the angles of any triangle is 180°. The 2 given angle measures total 70°. So, the missing angle measure is 180° − 70° = 110°.

7. D

The area of a square is s^2. Since the area is 49, a side measures 7. The perimeter is the sum of the lengths of the sides: 4 times 7 = 28.

8. D

The sum of supplementary angles is 180°.

9. C

A straight angle measures 180°. The described angles would be x and $9 + 2x$. An equation for this is: $x + 9 + 2x = 180$. This simplifies to $3x + 9 = 180$, or $3x = 171$. Thus, x measures 57°. The other angle measures $9 + 2x$, which is $9 + 2(57) = 9 + 114 = 123$. The larger angle measures 123°.

10. C

The perimeter of a polygon is the sum of the lengths of the sides. This square has a perimeter of $4(5) = 20$.

11. D

The area of a rectangle is the length times the width: 7 times 10 = 70.

12. B

The sum of the measures of the angles of any quadrilateral (a polygon with 4 sides) is 360°.

13. C

The origin is (0,0). The other point is $(-8, 6)$. Average the x's and the y's to get the midpoint.

14. C

An isosceles right triangle has 1 right angle, measuring 90°, and 2 congruent acute angles. So, since any triangle has a total of 180° in its interior angles, the 2 congruent angle measures must total 90° (180° − 90°). Then, divide 90° by 2 to get the measure of each congruent angle, which ends up being 45°.

15. D

The sum of supplementary angles is 180°.

16. B

Also, a diameter is made of 2 radii. An arc is a portion of a circle. A semi-circle is half of a circle.

17. C

Use the Pythagorean Theorem: $\text{leg}_1^2 + \text{leg}_2^2 = h^2$. That would be $12^2 + 9^2 = c^2$. Thus, $144 + 81 = c^2$, which is $225 = c^2$, making $c = 15$.

18. D

Add the measures of all of the sides of a polygon to get its perimeter. Length + 2 + length + 2 = 20. 2(length) + 4 = 20. 2(length) = 16 and length = 8. The length of this rectangle measures 8 dm.

19. C

The area of a square is s^2. Since the area is 144, a side measures 12. The perimeter is the sum of the lengths of the sides: 4 times 12 = 48. The perimeter is 48 inches.

20. A

The sum of the angles of any triangle is 180°. Since a right angle measures 90°, the measure of the remaining 2 angles in a right triangle is 90°. If 1 of these angles measures 73°, then the other measures 90° − 73°, or 17°.

Algebra 1 EOC
Practice Test

Algebra 1 and Geometry End-of-Course Assessments Reference Sheet

Area

Parallelogram $\quad A = bh$

Triangle $\quad A = \frac{1}{2}bh$

Trapezoid $\quad A = \frac{1}{2}h(b_1 + b_2)$

Circle $\quad A = \pi r^2$

Regular Polygon $\quad A = \frac{1}{2}aP$

KEY

b = base	A = area
h = height	B = area of base
w = width	C = circumference
d = diameter	V = volume
r = radius	P = perimeter
ℓ = slant height	of base
a = apothem	$S.A.$ = surface area

Use 3.14 or $\frac{22}{7}$ for π.

Circumference
$C = \pi d \quad \text{or} \quad C = 2\pi r$

		Volume/Capacity	Total Surface Area
	Rectangular Prism	$V = bwh$ or $V = Bh$	$S.A. = 2bh + 2bw + 2hw$ or $S.A. = Ph + 2B$
	Right Circular Cylinder	$V = \pi r^2 h$ or $V = Bh$	$S.A. = 2\pi rh + 2\pi r^2$ or $S.A. = 2\pi rh + 2B$
	Right Square Pyramid	$V = \frac{1}{3}Bh$	$S.A. = \frac{1}{2}P\ell + B$
	Right Circular Cone	$V = \frac{1}{3}\pi r^2 h$ or $V = \frac{1}{3}Bh$	$S.A. = \frac{1}{2}(2\pi r)\ell + B$
	Sphere	$V = \frac{4}{3}\pi r^3$	$S.A. = 4\pi r^2$

Sum of the measures of the interior angles of a polygon $= 180(n-2)$

Measure of an interior angle of a regular polygon $= \dfrac{180(n-2)}{n}$

where:

n represents the number of sides

Algebra 1 and Geometry End-of-Course Assessments Reference Sheet

Slope formula

$$m = \frac{y_2 - y_1}{x_2 - x_1}$$

where m = slope and (x_1, y_1) and (x_2, y_2) are points on the line

Slope-intercept form of a linear equation

$$y = mx + b$$

where m = slope and b = y-intercept

Point-slope form of a linear equation

$$y - y_1 = m(x - x_1)$$

where m = slope and (x_1, y_1) is a point on the line

Distance between two points

$P_1(x_1, y_1)$ and $P_2(x_2, y_2)$

$$\sqrt{(x_2 - x_1)^2 + (y_2 - y_1)^2}$$

Midpoint between two points

$P_1(x_1, y_1)$ and $P_2(x_2, y_2)$

$$\left(\frac{x_1 + x_2}{2} , \frac{y_1 + y_2}{2} \right)$$

Quadratic formula

$$x = \frac{-b \pm \sqrt{b^2 - 4ac}}{2a}$$

where a, b, and c are coefficients in an equation of the form $ax^2 + bx + c = 0$

Special Right Triangles

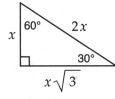 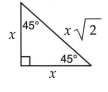

Trigonometric Ratios

$$\sin A° = \frac{\text{opposite}}{\text{hypotenuse}}$$

$$\cos A° = \frac{\text{adjacent}}{\text{hypotenuse}}$$

$$\tan A° = \frac{\text{opposite}}{\text{adjacent}}$$

Conversions

1 yard = 3 feet
1 mile = 1,760 yards = 5,280 feet
1 acre = 43,560 square feet
1 hour = 60 minutes
1 minute = 60 seconds

1 cup = 8 fluid ounces
1 pint = 2 cups
1 quart = 2 pints
1 gallon = 4 quarts
1 pound = 16 ounces
1 ton = 2,000 pounds

1 meter = 100 centimeters = 1000 millimeters
1 kilometer = 1000 meters
1 liter = 1000 milliliters = 1000 cubic centimeters
1 gram = 1000 milligrams
1 kilogram = 1000 grams

Directions for Taking Algebra I EOC Practice Test A

Test Questions

This Practice Test contains 51 questions. The number of questions on the actual test will vary.

- ### Multiple-Choice Questions

    Select the best answer for each question and mark it on the answer sheet on page 258.

- ### Open-ended Questions

    As you come to an open-ended question, use the Notes pages at the back of the book to do your work. Then fill in the answer using the digits 0-9 and/or the symbols for a decimal point, fraction bar, or negative sign in the answer box provided for each specific open-ended question.

Reference Pages

You may refer to the two preceding Reference Pages as often as you like.

Timing

For the actual test you will be given two 80-minute periods to complete the test, with a ten-minute break in between. However, anyone who has not finished will be allowed to continue working.

Checking Your Answers

You will find the correct answers, along with detailed explanations, for this practice test beginning on page 260.

Reviewing Your Work

When finished, turn to the grid on page 306. Circle the number of any questions that you missed in Test A. You will be able to see a pattern that shows which Benchmarks will need your further attention.

1 At the discount shopping center, the cost of mangos is constant. The total price increases as the number of mangos purchased increases. The table below shows the price in dollars for several quantities of mangos.

PRICE OF MANGOS

Number of Mangos Purchased	Price in Dollars
2	$1.50
3	$2.25
4	$3.00
5	$3.75
6	$4.50

Which equation represents p, the price in dollars, as a function of n, of the number of mangos purchased?

A. $p = .15n$

B. $p = 1.5n$

C. $p = .75n$

D. $p = 7.5n$

2 At Minerva's Miniature Golf World the cost for a child's birthday party is $50.00 plus $7.50 for each child attending. The function below can be used to determine $f(n)$, the total cost of the party for n children.

$F(n) = 50 + 7.5n$

If the total cost for a birthday party is $177.50, what was the total number of children attending the party?

Go On ▶

3 The set of ordered pairs shown below defines a relation.

$\{(-7, 2), (4, -5), (1, 8), (-3, 9), (0, 7)\}$

What is the **domain** of this relation?

A. $\{-7, -3, 1, 4\}$

B. $\{-7, -3, 0, 1, 4\}$

C. $\{-5, 1, 2, 3, 7, 9\}$

D. $\{-5, 2, 3, 7, 8, 9\}$

4 The graph below represents the daily average temperatures for a recent week on an island in the Florida Keys. The horizontal axis is measured in days, and the vertical axis is measures in degrees Celsius.

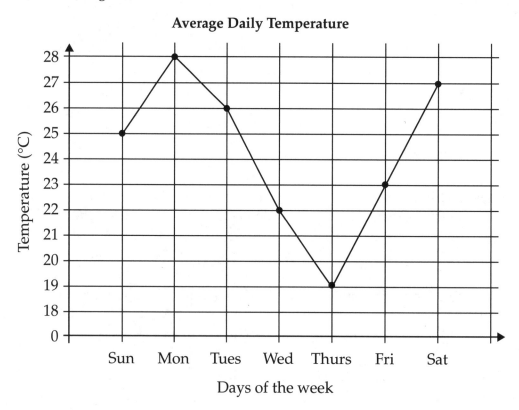

Average Daily Temperature

Based on the graph, which of the following best describes the **range** of the temperature for this week, where x represents the temperature?

F. $19 \leq x \leq 27$

G. $19 \leq x \leq 28$

H. $25 \leq x \leq 27$

I. $25 \leq x \leq 28$

5 The graph below represents a quadratic function.

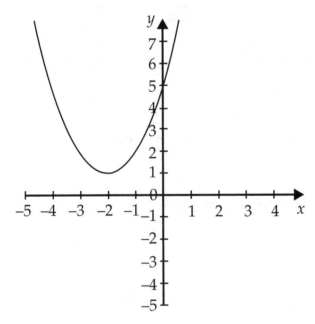

Based on the graph, what is the least element in the range of this function?

Go On

6 Elaine has three types of nuts, peanuts, cashews and almonds, that she combines and stores in a large container. There are three times as many ounces of peanuts as of cashews. There are 5 more ounces of almonds than cashews. The total weight of the mixed nuts is 20 ounces. How many ounces are there of peanuts?

7 Jorge and his brother Marcos are going to meet their parents at their beach vacation cottage. Jorge leaves their home 2 hours earlier than Marcos and rides his scooter. His average speed is 20 miles per hour. Marcos also leaves from their home and drives his car along the same route as Jorge. His average sped is 40 miles per hour. The equation below can be used to model this situation, where t represents the time that has elapsed since Jorge left home.

$$20t = 40(t - 2)$$

What will be the distance, in miles, when Marcos catches up with Jorge?

8 The formula for the area of a trapezoid can be written as

$$A = \frac{h}{2}(a+b)$$

Where a and b are the lengths of the parallel sides, and h is the height. Which of the following shows the formula solved for a?

F. $a = \dfrac{2A - b}{h}$

G. $a = \dfrac{2A - hb}{h}$

H. $a = 2A - b - h$

I. $a = 2A - 2b - 2h$

Go On ▶

9 Tameka is planning to prepare an area for a rectangular vegetable garden. She has 260 feet of wire fencing she can use to enclose the garden. She will use the side of an existing fence for one side of the garden. The existing fence is 40 feet long, and she wants to use the whole 40 feet for one side. Tameka used the following inequality to calculate the maximum length of the garden.

$2L + 40 \le 260$

Which of the following is the solution to this inequality?

A. $L \le 70$

B. $L \le 110$

C. $L \le 130$

D. $L \le 150$

10 Which graph is the solution to the inequality shown below?

$-8 \le 6x - 4(x - 3) \le 2$

F.

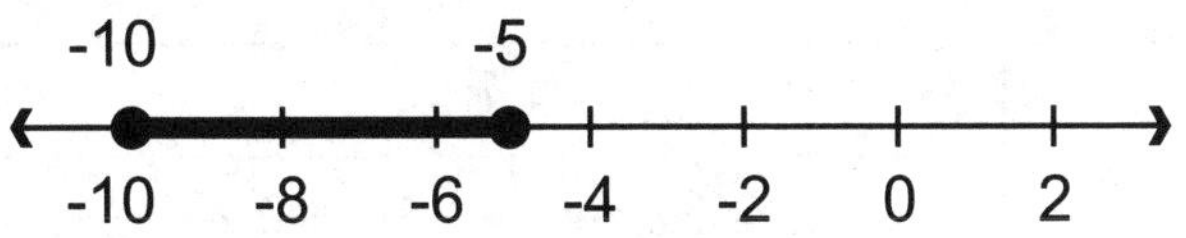

G.

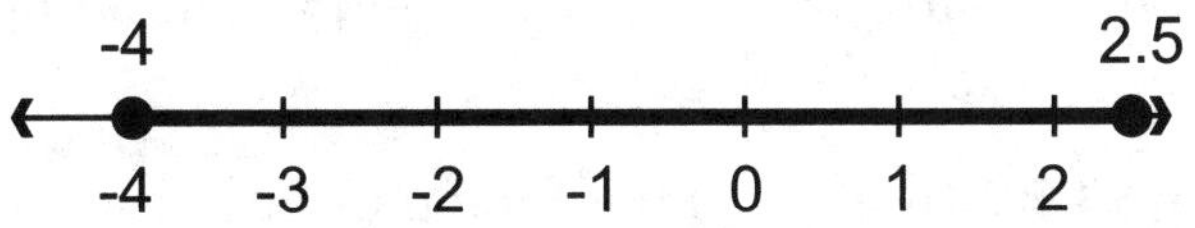

H.

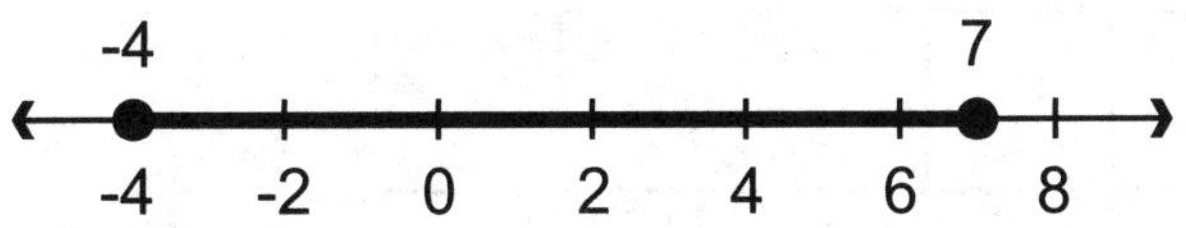

I.

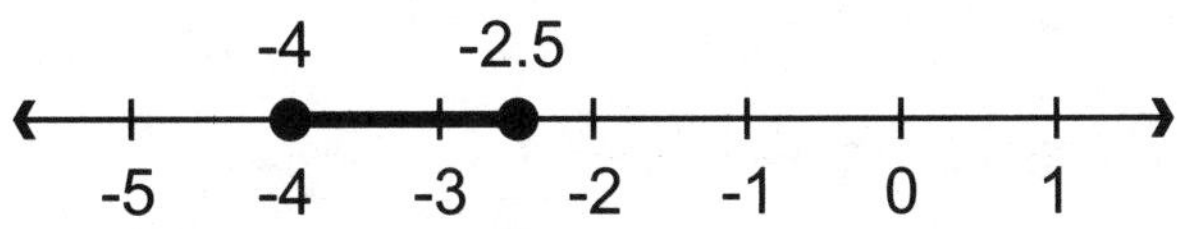

Go On

11 A rental car company charges a fee of $100 for one week plus $.10 a mile for every mile over 50 miles (before taxes and other fees) when the car is returned. Richard rents a car for one week and drives more than 50 miles during that week. If x represents the total number of miles Richard drove and C represents the charge before taxes and other fees, which of the following equations can be used to determine Richard's charge before taxes and other fees?

A. $C = 100 + 10x$

B. $C = 100 + .10x$

C. $C = 100 + 10\,(x - 50)$

D. $C = 100 + .10\,(x - 50)$

12 Ashley works in a retail store at the mall. Her monthly salary is calculated using the equations shown in the following table.

MONTHLY EARNINGS EQUATION

Total Sales for the Month (s in dollars)	Earnings Equation
$s \le \$3,500$	$E = 2,500 + 0.1s$
$s > \$3,500$	$E = \$2,500 + 0.1s + 0.2(s - 3500)$

where **E** represents Ashley's total monthly earnings before taxes and withholding, and *s* represents the dollar amount of Ashley's total sales.

Ashley's total sales were greater than $3,500 in June. If her total monthly earnings for June were $3,900, what was the value of her total monthly sales *s*?

Go On ▶

13 Lilly went to the pet store and bought millet seeds and sunflower seeds for her cockatiels. Millet seeds sold for $5.00 a pound and sunflower seeds for $2.50 a pound. Lilly spent $15.00 for her purchase. The equation below can be used to determine how many pounds of each seed Lilly bought, where x is the number of pounds of millet seeds and y is the number of pounds of sunflower seeds Lilly bought.

$5x + 2.5y = 15.00$

Which of the following shows the graph of this equation?

A.

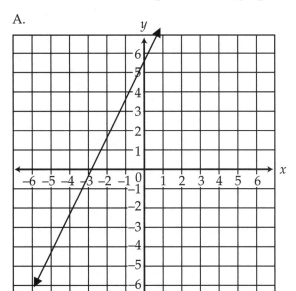

C.

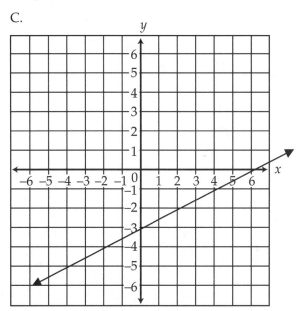

B.

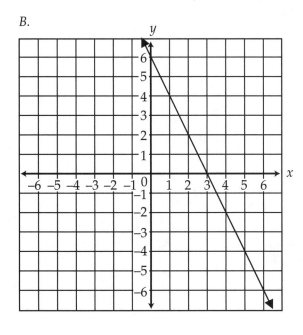

D.

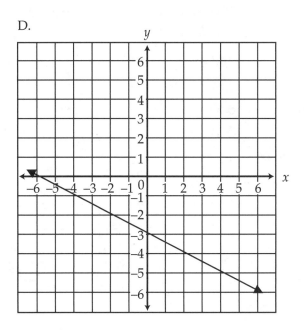

Go On

14 As a group of hikers climb Mount Hood in Oregon, they notice that the temperature drops 5 degrees for every 1,000-foot increase in elevation. The relationship between the increase in elevation and decrease in temperature can be modeled by the equation.

$5x + 1000y = 0$ where x is measured in feet and y is measured in degrees.

Which of the following represents the slope of the equation?

F. $-\dfrac{1}{20}$

G. $-\dfrac{1}{200}$

H. $\dfrac{1}{20}$

I. $\dfrac{1}{200}$

15 A train going from Jacksonville, Florida, to Washington, D.C., travels at a constant rate. The graph of the line below represents the relationship between time in hours and distance traveled. The line passes through (0,0) and (15, 350).

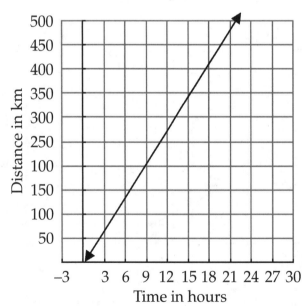

DISTANCE FROM JACKSONVILLE

What is the slope of the line shown? Round off to the nearest tenth.

16 In Jacob's geometry class he drew the following triangle in the coordinate plane.

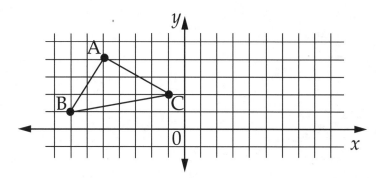

Jacob determined that the coordinates of point A were $(-5, 4)$ and the coordinates of point C were $(-1, 2)$.

Which of the following equations best represents the line that contains the points A and C?

F. $y = -\dfrac{1}{2}x - \dfrac{1}{2}$

G. $y = -\dfrac{1}{2}x + 3$

H. $y = -\dfrac{1}{2}x + \dfrac{3}{2}$

I. $y = -2x - 6$

Go On

17   On the coordinate grid below the two lines, l_1 and l_2, are parallel. Line l_1 contains the points $(5, 0)$ and $(0, 2)$.

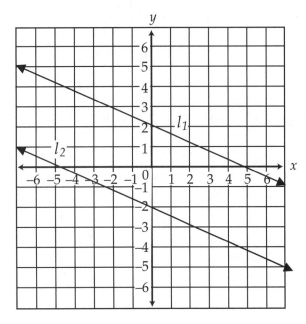

What is the slope of line l_2?

18   Which of the following pairs of lines whose equations are given are perpendicular?

F. $2x + 3y = 10$

   $3x + 2y = 5$

G. $2x - 3y = 10$

   $3x + 2y = 5$

H. $3x - 2y = 10$

   $2x - 3y = 5$

I. $2x - 3y = 10$

   $2x + 3y = 5$

19 Tony is opening a taco stand during lunch hours near the courthouse. He keeps track of the number of tacos sold each day during the first week and makes a scatter plot. Then he draws a line of best fit on the scatter plot, as shown below.

Taco Sales, Week One

Which statement best expresses the meaning of the slope as a rate of change for this line of best fit?

A. It represents the number of tacos he will have to sell to make a profit.

B. It represents the number of tacos he will sell the next week.

C. It represents the increase in number of tacos sold each day after opening.

D. It represents the average number of tacos sold each day.

Go On ▶

20 Isabella graphed the line shown below on the coordinate plane. The line passes through the points $(0, 5)$ and $(1, 3)$.

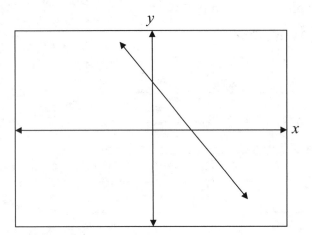

What is the x-coordinate at which this line intersects the x-axis?

21 Maurice bought 3 sodas and 4 candy bars for $10.17. Larry bought 2 sodas and 5 candy bars for $10.28.

Which statement shows the cost of each soda and each candy bar?

A. Each soda costs $1.29 and each candy bar costs $1.49.

B. Each soda costs $1.29 and each candy bar costs $1.50.

C. Each soda costs $1.39 and each candy bar costs $1.50.

D. Each soda costs $1.39 and each candy bar costs $1.59.

22 The Shakespeare Playhouse charges $24.00 for adult tickets and $12.50 for student tickets. The total sales was $403.50 and 24 tickets were sold. Several families and their children, all high school students, attended a production at the play house. The set of equations below describes this situation, where x is the number of adults who attended and y is the number of students who attended.

$24x + 12.5y = 403.5$

$x + y = 24$

What is the exact number of students who attended?

23 The expression $(ab^4c^{-2})^5$ is equivalent to which of the following?

A. $5ab^9c^3$

B. $a^5b^{20}c^{10}$

C. $5ab^{20}c^{-10}$

D. $a^5b^{20}c^{-10}$

24 Juan simplified the expression shown below.

$(x^3y^7z^{-3})(x^6y^{-4}z)$

His final answer was in the form $x^my^nz^p$. If he simplified the expression correctly, what is the value of p, the exponent of z?

Go On ▶

25   Adam simplified the expression shown below.

$(p^{-4}q^4)^{-3}$

His final answer was in the form $p^m q^n$. If he simplified the expression correctly, what is the exponent of p?

26   Janet is planning to cover the floor of her rectangular patio with artificial turf. The sides are x feet in width, and the length is 4 feet longer than twice the width, $2x + 4$. In terms of x, what is the area in square feet of Janet's patio?

   F. $6x + 8$

   G. $6x + 16$

   H. $2x^2 + 4x$

   I. $2x^2 + 8$

27   A square has sides of length s. If the sides are all increased by 5 units, how much larger is the perimeter of the larger square compared to the perimeter of the original square?

   A.   5

   B.   20

   C. $s + 5$

   D. $5s$

Go On

28 Marcia multiplied the following polynomials and simplified her results:

$(3x + 2)(4x - 3)$

Which of the following terms appears in her answer, after she has simplified?

F. $7x^2$

G. $12x^2$

H. x

I. 6

29 The band, chorus and string orchestra at a high school are selling candy bars to raise money for a trip to the Orange Bowl. If x represents the profit from selling one candy bar, then the following expression represents how much money they raised:

$bx + (cx + sx)$

Which of the following expressions is equivalent to the expression above?

A. $b + (c + s)x$

B. $(b + c) + sx$

C. $3(b + c + s)x$

D. $(b + c + s)x$

30 A fisherman accidentally drops his soda can off the 25-foot-high pier at Daytona Beach. The height of the soda can after t seconds is given by the polynomial $25 - 16t^2$. Which of the following is equivalent to this polynomial?

F. $(5 - 4t)(5 - 4t)$

G. $(5 - 4t)(5 + 4t)$

H. $(5t - 4)(5t + 4)$

I. $(5t - 4)(5t - 4)$

Go On ▶

31 If $x \neq -2$, which of the following shows the expression below in simplest form?

$$\frac{2x^2 - 2x - 12}{x + 2}$$

A. $2x - 3$

B. $2(x - 3)$

C. $2(x + 3)$

D. $x + 2$

32 Ishaan needs to simplify the following expression before he uses it in a computation.

$$\frac{x^{16}y^{12} + x^8y^6}{x^4y^2}$$

If $x \neq 0$ and $y \neq 0$, which of the following is a simplified version of the expression above?

F. x^6y^9

G. $x^{20}y^{16}$

H. $x^4y^6 + x^2y^3$

I. $x^{12}y^{10} + x^4y^4$

33 The legend on an architect's scale drawing of a building indicates that 1.5 inches = 50 feet. If the building in the drawing is 10.25 inches tall, how tall in feet will the building be when built? Round off your answer to the nearest tenth.

Go On

34 The following are similar triangles.

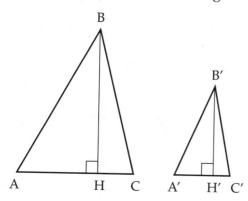

The lengths of the following sides are given:

length of side AB = 18 cm

length of side BC = 12 cm

length of side AC = 9 cm

length of side A′B′ = 15 cm

What is the length in cm. of side B′C′ ?

35 What is the solution of the equation below?

$$\frac{4}{x-6} = \frac{5}{2x}$$

A. $x = 2$

B. $x = 6$

C. $x = -10$

D. $x = -30$

Go On ▶

36 Felicia simplified the following expression in her algebra class.

$$\sqrt{5}\left(\sqrt{10}+2\sqrt{30}\right)$$

If Felicia simplified correctly, which of the following is her answer?

F. $15\sqrt{18}$

G. $7\sqrt{40}$

H. $5\sqrt{2}+10\sqrt{6}$

I. $5\sqrt{10}+10\sqrt{30}$

37 Joanna needs to divide and simplify the following expression in order to finish her homework. Assume a and b are greater than 0.

$$\frac{\sqrt{9a^2b}}{\sqrt{3b}}$$

If she simplifies correctly, which of the following will be her answer?

A. $a\sqrt{3}$

B. $3ab$

C. $9a$

D. $2a\sqrt{b}$

38 Julian worked the following problem by performing the subtraction and simplifying before he left for soccer practice. Assume x is greater than 0.

$$3\sqrt{18x} - 7\sqrt{8x}$$

If he worked the problem correctly, which of the following is his answer?

F. $\sqrt{2x}$

G. $-\sqrt{2x}$

H. $-5\sqrt{2x}$

I. $-8\sqrt{2x}$

39 Rosalie added and simplified the following radical expressions.

$$\sqrt{12} + 7\sqrt{45} + 3\sqrt{20}$$

If she added and simplified correctly, which of the following is her answer?

A. $31\sqrt{5}$

B. $2\sqrt{3} + 24\sqrt{5}$

C. $3\sqrt{2} + 27\sqrt{5}$

D. $2\sqrt{3} + 27\sqrt{5}$

Go On

40 Which of the following is the graph of $y = x^2 - 10x + 25$?

F.

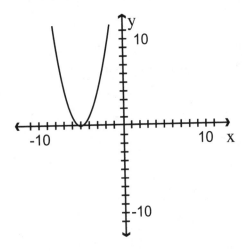

G.

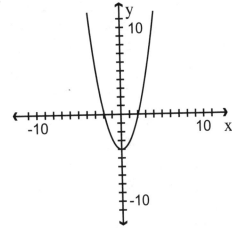

H.

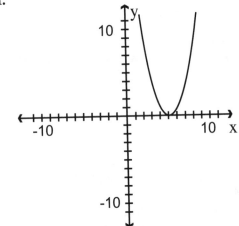

I.

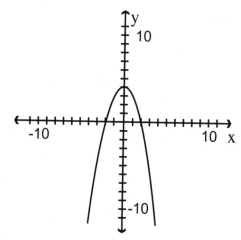

41 Thelma correctly solved the quadratic equation shown by factoring.

$x^2 + 5x - 6 = 0$

Which of the following shows a step in solving this equation?

A. $(x + 2)(x - 3)$

B. $(x - 2)(x + 3)$

C. $(x + 1)(x - 6)$

D. $(x - 1)(x + 6)$

42 Fred completed his homework by using factoring to solve the following quadratic equation.

$2x^2 + 7x = 4$

If he solved the equation correctly, which of the following are the solutions he found?

F. $\frac{1}{2}, -4$

G. $-\frac{1}{2}, 4$

H. $2, -4$

I. $-2, 4$

Go On ➤

43 Charlene solved the following polynomial using factoring.

$4x^2 - 100 = 0$

If she solved the equation correctly, which of the following are the solutions she found?

A. $-2, 2$

B. $-4, 4$

C. $-5, 5$

D. $-10, 10$

44 A model rocket is launched vertically in the air. The equation that gives its height h, in feet above the ground in t seconds is given below.

$h = 320t - 16t^2$

What is the total elapsed time, in seconds, from the time the rocket is launched until it hits the ground?

45 The set S represents the set of all sandwiches offered for sale at a concession stand.

$S = \{$hamburger, hot dog, grilled cheese, veggieburger$\}$

The set C represents the set of all condiments available at the stand.

$C = \{$catsup, mustard, mayonnaise, relish, chopped onions$\}$

What is the total number of elements in the set $S \times C$?

Go On

46 Let *E* represent the set of even whole numbers.

$E = \{0, 2, 4, 6, 8, \ldots\}$

Let the set *A* be defined as follows.

$A = \{8, 10, 12, \ldots\}$

What is the complement of *A*, ~*A*, in *E*?

F. $\{0, 2, 4, 6, 8, \ldots\}$

G. $\{8, 10, 12, 14, 16, \ldots\}$

H. $\{0, 2, 4, 6, 8\}$

I. $\{0, 2, 4, 6\}$

47 The set *T* represents Tom's favorite sports programs.

T = {baseball, basketball, golf, soccer}

The set *H* represents Helen's favorite sports programs.

H = {baseball, football, soccer, tennis}

Which set below represents $H \cup T$?

A. {baseball, soccer}

B. {baseball, basketball, football}

C. {basketball, football, golf, tennis}

D. {baseball, basketball, football, golf, soccer, tennis}

Go On ▶

48   Sarah's scores on the first six algebra quizzes are represented in set *S*.

$S = \{7, 9, 10, 9.2, 7.5, 8\}$

Matt's scores on the first six algebra quizzes are represented in set *M*.

$M = \{10, 6, 7.8, 8, 9, 9.2\}$

Cleo's scores on the first six algebra quizzes are represented in set *C*.

$C = \{7, 7.5, 8.2, 8.8, 9, 10\}$

Which set below represents $S \cap (M \cup C)$?

F. $\{8, 9, 9.2, 10\}$

G. $\{7, 7.5, 8, 9, 10\}$

H. $\{7, 7.5, 8, 9, 9.2, 10\}$

I. $\{6, 7, 7.7, 7.8, 8, 8.2, 8.8, 9, 9.2, 10\}$

49   The universal set contains only sets *R*, *S*, and *T*. These sets are related as shown in the Venn diagram below.

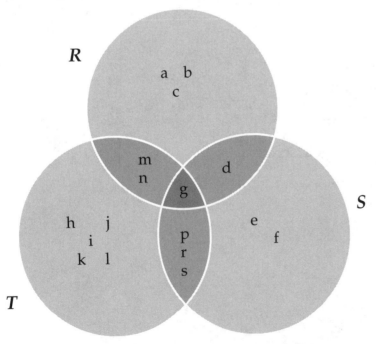

Which set represents $S \cap (\sim R \cup T)$?

A. {g, p, r, s}

B. {e, f, g, p, r, s}

C. {a, b, c, m, n, h, i, j, k, l}

D. { a, b, c, m, n, g, h, i, j, k, l}

50 Martha conducted a survey to determine the favorite music of students at her school. The Venn Diagram below shows the number of students who chose one of the categories shown.

FAVORITE MUSIC CHOICES

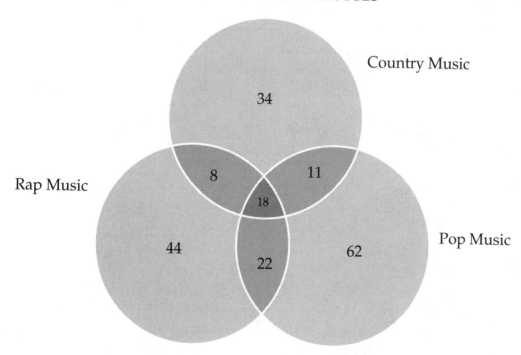

Based on the diagram, what is the total number of students who do NOT like country music?

Go On ▶

51 The graph below represents the system of equations

$3x + 2y = 11$

$4x - 3y = 9$

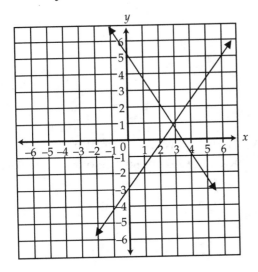

What is the solution of this system?

A. $(-3, 1)$

B. $(1, 3)$

C. $(2, 3)$

D. $(3, 1)$

This is the end of the Mathematics Test.

Until time is called, go back and check your work or answer questions
you did not complete. When you have finished, close your
Test Book and Answer Book.

Algebra Practice Test Form A

Answer Sheet

1. Ⓐ Ⓑ Ⓒ Ⓓ

2. ☐☐☐☐☐☐

3. Ⓐ Ⓑ Ⓒ Ⓓ

4. Ⓕ Ⓖ Ⓗ Ⓘ

5. ☐☐☐☐☐☐

6. ☐☐☐☐☐☐

7. ☐☐☐☐☐☐

8. Ⓕ Ⓖ Ⓗ Ⓘ

9. Ⓐ Ⓑ Ⓒ Ⓓ

10. Ⓕ Ⓖ Ⓗ Ⓘ

11. Ⓐ Ⓑ Ⓒ Ⓓ

12. ☐☐☐☐☐☐☐

13. Ⓐ Ⓑ Ⓒ Ⓓ

14. Ⓕ Ⓖ Ⓗ Ⓘ

15. ☐☐☐☐☐☐

16. Ⓕ Ⓖ Ⓗ Ⓘ

17. ☐☐☐☐☐☐

18. Ⓕ Ⓖ Ⓗ Ⓘ

19. Ⓐ Ⓑ Ⓒ Ⓓ

20. ☐☐☐☐☐☐

21. Ⓐ Ⓑ Ⓒ Ⓓ

22. ☐☐☐☐☐☐

23. Ⓐ Ⓑ Ⓒ Ⓓ

24. ☐☐☐☐☐☐

25. ☐☐☐☐☐☐

26. Ⓕ Ⓖ Ⓗ Ⓘ

27. Ⓐ Ⓑ Ⓒ Ⓓ

28. Ⓕ Ⓖ Ⓗ Ⓘ

29. Ⓐ Ⓑ Ⓒ Ⓓ

30. Ⓕ Ⓖ Ⓗ Ⓘ

31. Ⓐ Ⓑ Ⓒ Ⓓ

32. Ⓕ Ⓖ Ⓗ Ⓘ

33. ☐☐☐☐☐☐

34. ☐☐☐☐☐☐

35. Ⓐ Ⓑ Ⓒ Ⓓ

36. Ⓕ Ⓖ Ⓗ Ⓘ

37. Ⓐ Ⓑ Ⓒ Ⓓ

38. Ⓕ Ⓖ Ⓗ Ⓘ

39. Ⓐ Ⓑ Ⓒ Ⓓ

40. Ⓕ Ⓖ Ⓗ Ⓘ

41. Ⓐ Ⓑ Ⓒ Ⓓ

42. Ⓕ Ⓖ Ⓗ Ⓘ

43. Ⓐ Ⓑ Ⓒ Ⓓ

44. ☐☐☐☐☐☐

45. ☐☐☐☐☐☐

46. Ⓕ Ⓖ Ⓗ Ⓘ

47. Ⓐ Ⓑ Ⓒ Ⓓ

48. Ⓕ Ⓖ Ⓗ Ⓘ

49. Ⓐ Ⓑ Ⓒ Ⓓ

50. ☐☐☐☐☐☐

51. Ⓐ Ⓑ Ⓒ Ⓓ

Go On ▶

Answers
Practice Test

Practice Test Form A: Answers and Explanations

1 **The answer is C.**
It is given in the table that 2 mangos cost $1.50. Divide this number by 2 to determine the cost of 1 mango, which yields $.75 for one mango. Thus, the equation is $p = .75n$.

2 **The answer is 17.**
Replacing $f(n)$ by 177.50 in the expression for the function results in

$177.50 = 50 + 7.5n$

Solving this equation for n, we add -50 to each side:

$177.50 - 50 = 50 - 50 + 7.5n$

Simplify each side of the equals sign:

$127.50 = 7.5n$

Divide both sides of the equation by 7.5 to obtain

$n = 17$

3 **The answer is B.**
The domain of the relation is the set of all first elements in the ordered pairs.

4 **The answer is G.**
The range is the set of all values on the vertical axis represented on the graph. The lowest value is 19, the highest value is 28, and all values in between correspond to the second coordinate of a point on a linear segment of the graph.

5 **The answer is 1.**
The lowest point on the graph appears to occur at the point $(-2, 1)$. The least element in the range is the second coordinate of the lowest point on the graph.

6 **The answer is 9 ounces.**

If x represents the amount of cashews, $3x$ represents the amount of peanuts, and $x + 5$ represents the amount of almonds. The equation to solve is

$$3x + x + x + 5 = 20.$$
$$5x + 5 = 20$$
$$5x = 15$$
$$x = 3 \text{ the amount of cashews.}$$

The amount of peanuts is $3x = 3(3) = 9$ ounces.

7 **The answer is 80 miles.**

Solve the given equation:

$$20t = 40(t - 2)$$
$$20t = 40t - 80$$
$$80 = 20t$$

$t = 4$ hours. This represents the time Marcos spends before he catches up. The distance is 4 hours $\times$ 20 miles per hour = 80 miles.

8 **The answer is G.**

$$\text{Solve } A = h/2(a + b)$$

First, multiply both sides by 2. $\qquad 2A = h(a + b)$
Remove parentheses: $\qquad\qquad 2A = ha + hb$
Subtract hb from both sides: $\qquad 2A - hb = ha$
Divide both sides by h: $\qquad (2A - hb)/h = a$

9 **The answer is B.**

Solve the inequality $\quad 2L + 40 \leq 260$

Add -40 to both sides $\qquad 2L \leq 220$
Divide both sides by 2 $\qquad\quad L \leq 110$

10 **The answer is F.**

Solve the compound inequality
$$-8 \leq 6x - 4(x - 3) \leq 2$$
Remove parentheses: $\qquad\quad -8 \leq 6x - 4x + 12 \leq 2$
Combine like terms: $\qquad\qquad -8 \leq 2x + 12 \leq 2$
Add -12 to all three parts: $\quad -8 - 12 \leq 2x + 12 - 12 \leq 2 - 12$

Go On

Combine like terms: $-20 \leq 2x \leq -10$
Divide all three parts by 2: $-10 \leq x \leq -5$

11 **The answer is D.**
The cost is $100 plus $.10 for every mile over 50, which is $(x - 50)$. Thus, the cost is $100 + $.10 times $(x - 50)$.

12 **The answer is $7,000.**
Let E = 3,900 in the equation for $s > 3,500$ and solve for s:
$$3900 = 2500 + .1s + .2(s - 3500)$$
Remove parentheses: $3900 = 2500 + .1s + .2s - 700$
Combine like terms: $3900 = 1800 + .3s.$
Add -1800 to both sides: $3900 - 1800 = 1800 - 1800 + .3s$
$$2100 = .3s$$
Divide both sides by .3: $7000 = s$

13 **The answer is B.**
Find the x- and y-intercepts of the line: Let $x = 0$ in the equation $5x + 2.5y = 15.00$
$2.5y = 15$ $0 + 2.5y = 15$
Divide both sides by 2.5: $y = 6$ Thus, $(0, 6)$ is the y-intercept.
Let $y = 0$: $5x + 0 = 15$
$5x = 15$
Divide both sides by 5: $x = 3$ Thus $(3, 0)$ is the x-intercept.
The graph goes through these two points.

14 **The answer is G.**
Solve the equation $5x + 1000y = 0$ for y:
Add $-5x$ both sides: $1000y = -5x$
Divide both sides by 1000: $y = \dfrac{-5}{1000}x$
Reduce the coefficient of x: $y = \dfrac{-1}{200}x$
The slope is the coefficient of x: $\dfrac{-1}{200}$ The decimal equivalent is $-.005$.

15 The answer is $\dfrac{70}{3}$.

The decimal equivalent is $23.\overline{3}$

Use the formula for slope $m = \dfrac{y_1 - y_2}{x_1 - x_2}$, using the points $(0, 0)$ and $(15, 350)$:

Slope $= \dfrac{350 - 0}{15 - 0} = \dfrac{350}{15} = \dfrac{70}{3}$

16 The answer is H.

The slope of the line is $m = \dfrac{4 - 2}{-5 - (-1)} = \dfrac{2}{-4} = -\dfrac{1}{2}$ Using the point-slope equation,

$y - y_1 = m(x - x_1)$ with $m = -\dfrac{1}{2}$ and $(x_1, y_1) = (-5, 4)$, we have $y - 4 = -\dfrac{1}{2}(x - (-5))$

Remove parentheses: $y - 4 = -\dfrac{1}{2}x - \dfrac{5}{2}$

Add $+4$ to both sides: $y = -\dfrac{1}{2}x - \dfrac{5}{2} + \dfrac{8}{2}$

$y = -\dfrac{1}{2}x + \dfrac{3}{2}$

17 The answer is $-\dfrac{2}{5} = -0.4$.

The slope of line l_1 is $m = \dfrac{2 - 0}{0 - 5} = -\dfrac{2}{5}$. The slope of line l_2 is the same as the slope of line

l_1 because parallel lines have the same slope.

18 The answer is G.

Solve each equation for y to put the equations in slope-intercept form, $y = mx + b$

First equation: $2x - 3y = 10$

Add $-2x$ to both sides: $-3y = -2x + 10$

Divide both sides by -3: $y = \dfrac{2}{3}x - \dfrac{10}{3}$ Slope $= \dfrac{2}{3}$

Second equation: $3x + 2y = 5$

Add $-3x$ to both sides: $2y = -3x + 5$

Go On ▶

Divide both sides by 2:

$$y = \frac{-3}{2}x + \frac{5}{2} \qquad \text{Slope} = \frac{-3}{2}.$$

Two lines are perpendicular if the product of their slopes is -1, and $\frac{2}{3} \times \frac{-3}{2} = -1$.

19 **The answer is C.**

The slope as a rate of change is the increase or decrease in the range values, or tacos sold, compared to an increase in the domain values, days of the week. It indicates the increase (since the line is increasing and the slope is positive) in the number of tacos sold in one more day compared to the number sold the previous day.

20 **The answer is** $x = \dfrac{5}{2} = 2.5.$

The slope of the line is $m = \dfrac{3-5}{1-0} = -2$. Using the slope-intercept equation, $y = mx + b$, where $(0, b)$ is the y-intercept and m is the slope, we have $m = -2$ and $b = 5$. Thus, the equation of the line is $y = -2x + 5$. We let $y = 0$ in this equation and solve for x to find the x-intercept, which is the x-coordinate at which this line intersects the x-axis.

$0 = -2x + 5$
$2x = 5$
$x = \dfrac{5}{2} = 2.5$

21 **The answer is C.**

The answer is obtained by solving the system

$3x + 4y = 10.17$
$2x + 5y = 10.28$

Where x represents the price of a soda and y represents the cost of a candy bar. Multiply the first equation by -2, and multiply the second equation by 3, then add the equations together: $-6x - 8y = -20.34$
$6x + 15y = 30.84$
Add together to get: $7y = 10.5$
Divide both sides by 7: $y = 1.50$. The cost of a candy bar is \$1.50. Replace y by 1.5 in either of the original two equations to obtain $x = 1.39$:
$3x + 4(1.5) = 10.17$
$3x + 6 = 10.17$
Add -6 to both sides: $3x = 4.17$
Divide both sides by 3: $x = 1.39$ The cost of a soda is \$1.39.

Go On ▶

22 **The answer is 15 students.**

Solve the given system by substitution: Solve the second equation for y and substitute it in the first equation:

$24x + 12.5(24 - x) = 403.5$

Solve the resulting equation for x:

$24x + 300 - 12.5x = 403.5$

$11.5x = 103.5$

$x = 9$ There were 9 adults. The number of students is $24 - 9 = 15$. We could have eliminated the variable x first and obtained the same result.

23 **The answer is D.**

Using the laws of exponents, $(ab^4c^{-2})^5 = a^5(b^4)^5(c^{-2})^5 = a^5b^{20}c^{-10}$

24 **The answer is $p = -2$.**

Since $z^{-3}z^1 = z^{-3+1} = z^{-2}$.

25 **The answer is m = 12.**

Using the laws of exponents, $(p^{-4}q^4)^{-3} = (p^{-4})^{-3}(q^4)^{-3} = p^{12}q^{-12}$

26 **The answer is H.**

The area is represented by $x(2x + 4) = 2x^2 + 4x$

27 **The answer is B.**

5 units are added to each side, and the perimeter of a square is equal to 4 times the length of one side. Since each side is 5 units longer, the increase is $4 \times 5 = 20$ units.

28 **The answer is G.**

$(3x + 2)(4x - 3) = 12x^2 - 9x + 8x - 6 = 12x^2 - x - 6$

29 **The answer is D.**

$bx + (cx + sx) = bx + cx + sx = (b + c + s)x$ using the distributive property of real numbers.

Go On

30 **The answer is G.**

$25 - 16t^2 = 5^2 - (4t)^2 = (5 - 4t)(5 + 4t)$ using the formula for factoring the difference of two squares, $a^2 - b^2 = (a - b)(a + b)$

31 **The answer is B.**

Factoring the numerator and reducing, we get

$$\frac{2x^2 - 2x - 12}{x + 2} = \frac{2(x^2 - x - 6)}{x + 2} = \frac{2(x - 3)(x + 2)}{x + 2} = 2(x - 3)$$

32 **The answer is I.**

Using the laws of exponents,

$$\frac{x^{16}y^{12} + x^8y^6}{x^4y^2} = \frac{x^{16}y^{12}}{x^4y^2} + \frac{x^8y^6}{x^4y^2} = x^{16-4}y^{12-2} + x^{8-4}y^{6-2} = x^{12}y^{10} + x^4y^4$$

33 **The answer is 341.7 feet or $341\frac{2}{3}$ or $\frac{1025}{3}$.**

Solve the proportion: $\dfrac{1.5}{50} = \dfrac{10.25}{x}$

Cross multiply: $1.5x = (50)(10.25)$

Divide both sides by 1.5: $x = \dfrac{(50)(10.25)}{1.5}$ or $x = \dfrac{1025}{3} \approx 341.7$

34 **The length of B′C′ is 10 cm.**

Using similarity of triangles, solve the proportion: $\dfrac{18}{12} = \dfrac{15}{x}$

Reduce the ratio on the left: $\dfrac{3}{2} = \dfrac{15}{x}$

Cross multiply: $\qquad 3x = 30$

Divide both sides by 3: $\qquad x = 10$

35 **The answer is C.**

Cross multiply to get $(4)(2x) = (5)(x - 6)$

$\qquad\qquad\qquad 8x = 5x - 30$

Add $-5x$ to each side: $\quad 3x = -30$

Divide both sides by 3: $\quad x = -10$

Go On

36 **The answer is H.**
Using the properties of radicals,
$$\sqrt{5}\left(\sqrt{10}+2\sqrt{30}\right)=\sqrt{50}+2\sqrt{150}=\sqrt{2\times25}+2\sqrt{6\times25}=5\sqrt{2}+2\times5\sqrt{6}=5\sqrt{2}+10\sqrt{6}$$

37 **The answer is A.**

Using the properties of radicals, $\dfrac{\sqrt{9a^2b}}{\sqrt{3b}}=\sqrt{\dfrac{9a^2b}{3b}}=\sqrt{3a^2}=a\sqrt{3}$

38 **The answer is H.**
Using the properties of radicals, $3\sqrt{18x}-7\sqrt{8x}=$
$$3\sqrt{9\times2x}-7\sqrt{4\times2x}=3\times3\sqrt{2x}-7\times2\sqrt{2x}=9\sqrt{2x}-14\sqrt{2x}=-5\sqrt{2x}$$

39 **The answer is D.**
Using the properties of radicals,
$$\sqrt{12}+7\sqrt{45}+3\sqrt{20}=\sqrt{4\times3}+7\sqrt{9\times5}+3\sqrt{4\times5}=2\sqrt{3}+7\times3\sqrt{5}+3\times2\sqrt{5}=$$
$$2\sqrt{3}+21\sqrt{5}+6\sqrt{5}=2\sqrt{3}+27\sqrt{5}$$

40 **The answer is H.**
To find the x-intercepts solve the equation $x^2-10x+25=0$. Factor: $(x-5)(x-5)=0$. Set each factor equal 0 and solve to obtain $x=5$. Thus the only x-intercept is $(5,0)$. Graph H is the only graph with $(5,0)$ as an x-intercept.

41 **The answer is D.**
$(x-1)(x+6)=x^2+6x-x-6=x^2+5x-6.$

42 **The answer is F.**

Solve $2x^2+7x-4=0$ by factoring: $(2x-1)(x+4)=0$

Set each factor $=0$: $\qquad\qquad 2x-1=0 \quad$ or $\quad x+4=0$

Solve each equation: $\qquad\quad 2x=1 \quad$ or $\quad x=-4$

$$x=\frac{1}{2} \quad \text{or} \quad x=-4$$

Go On ▶

43 **The answer is C.**

Solve by factoring:	$4x^2 - 100 = 0$
Divide by 4:	$x^2 - 25 = 0$
Factor:	$(x - 5)(x + 5) = 0$
Set each factor $= 0$:	$x - 5 = 0$ or $x + 5 = 0$
	$x = 5$ or $x = -5$

44 **The answer is 20 seconds.**

Let the height $h = 0$ and solve the equation $0 = 320t - 16t^2$.

Factor: $0 = 16t(20 - t)$.

Set each factor $= 0$: $16t = 0$ or $20 - t = 0$

Solve each equation: $t = 0$ or $t = 20$ The rocket hits the ground after 20 seconds ($t = 0$ is when it lifts off).

45 **The total number is 4 × 5 = 20, the number of elements in S times the number of elements in C.**

46 **The answer is I.**

The complement of A is the set of all elements in E that are NOT in A, which are the first 4 even whole numbers.

47 **The answer is D. $H \cup T$ is the union of all elements in H and T.**

It includes all elements in both sets.

48 **The answer is H.**

The set $S \cap (M \cup C)$ is the set of all elements in S that can be found in the union of M and C, which includes all elements in M and C. Each element in S is in either M or C, so this set is the same as S. The order in which the elements are listed does not matter.

49 **The answer is B.**

The elements in $S \cap (\sim R \cup T)$ are those elements in S that are also in T. The set $\sim R \cup T$ contains T and the elements e and f in S (not in R). The intersection of S and this set is all the elements in the intersection of S and T, {g, p, r, s, e, f}.

Go On

50 The answer is **128 = 44 + 22 +62**, the sum of numbers in the Rap Music circle and the Pop Music circle that are not included in the overlap with the Country Music circle.

51 **The solution is D.**

The solution of the system is the ordered pair where the graphs of the lines intersect. The lines intersect at the point (3, 1). The solution may also be written $x = 3$, $y = 1$.

Algebra 1 EOC
Practice Test

Algebra 1 and Geometry End-of-Course Assessments Reference Sheet

Area

Parallelogram $\qquad A = bh$

Triangle $\qquad A = \frac{1}{2}bh$

Trapezoid $\qquad A = \frac{1}{2}h(b_1 + b_2)$

Circle $\qquad A = \pi r^2$

Regular Polygon $\qquad A = \frac{1}{2}aP$

KEY

b = base	A = area
h = height	B = area of base
w = width	C = circumference
d = diameter	V = volume
r = radius	P = perimeter
ℓ = slant height	of base
a = apothem	$S.A.$ = surface area

Use 3.14 or $\frac{22}{7}$ for π.

Circumference
$C = \pi d \quad \text{or} \quad C = 2\pi r$

Volume/Capacity   Total Surface Area

 Rectangular Prism $\quad V = bwh$ or $\quad S.A. = 2bh + 2bw + 2hw$ or
$V = Bh \qquad\qquad S.A. = Ph + 2B$

 Right Circular Cylinder $\quad V = \pi r^2 h$ or $\quad S.A. = 2\pi rh + 2\pi r^2$ or
$V = Bh \qquad\qquad S.A. = 2\pi rh + 2B$

 Right Square Pyramid $\quad V = \frac{1}{3}Bh \qquad S.A. = \frac{1}{2}P\ell + B$

 Right Circular Cone $\quad V = \frac{1}{3}\pi r^2 h$ or $\quad S.A. = \frac{1}{2}(2\pi r)\ell + B$
$V = \frac{1}{3}Bh$

 Sphere $\quad V = \frac{4}{3}\pi r^3 \qquad S.A. = 4\pi r^2$

Sum of the measures of the interior angles of a polygon $= 180(n-2)$

Measure of an interior angle of a regular polygon $= \dfrac{180(n-2)}{n}$

where:
   n represents the number of sides

272

Algebra 1 and Geometry End-of-Course Assessments Reference Sheet

Slope formula

$$m = \frac{y_2 - y_1}{x_2 - x_1}$$

where m = slope and (x_1, y_1) and (x_2, y_2) are points on the line

Slope-intercept form of a linear equation

$$y = mx + b$$

where m = slope and b = y-intercept

Point-slope form of a linear equation

$$y - y_1 = m(x - x_1)$$

where m = slope and (x_1, y_1) is a point on the line

Distance between two points

$P_1(x_1, y_1)$ and $P_2(x_2, y_2)$

$$\sqrt{(x_2 - x_1)^2 + (y_2 - y_1)^2}$$

Midpoint between two points

$P_1(x_1, y_1)$ and $P_2(x_2, y_2)$

$$\left(\frac{x_1 + x_2}{2} , \frac{y_1 + y_2}{2} \right)$$

Quadratic formula

$$x = \frac{-b \pm \sqrt{b^2 - 4ac}}{2a}$$

where a, b, and c are coefficients in an equation of the form $ax^2 + bx + c = 0$

Special Right Triangles

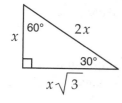 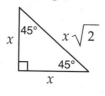

Trigonometric Ratios

$$\sin A° = \frac{\text{opposite}}{\text{hypotenuse}}$$

$$\cos A° = \frac{\text{adjacent}}{\text{hypotenuse}}$$

$$\tan A° = \frac{\text{opposite}}{\text{adjacent}}$$

Conversions

1 yard = 3 feet
1 mile = 1,760 yards = 5,280 feet
1 acre = 43,560 square feet
1 hour = 60 minutes
1 minute = 60 seconds

1 cup = 8 fluid ounces
1 pint = 2 cups
1 quart = 2 pints
1 gallon = 4 quarts
1 pound = 16 ounces
1 ton = 2,000 pounds

1 meter = 100 centimeters = 1000 millimeters
1 kilometer = 1000 meters
1 liter = 1000 milliliters = 1000 cubic centimeters
1 gram = 1000 milligrams
1 kilogram = 1000 grams

Directions for Taking Algebra I EOC Practice Test B

Test Questions

This Practice Test contains 51 questions. The number of questions on the actual test will vary.

- **Multiple-Choice Questions**

  Select the best answer for each question and mark it on the answer sheet on page 294.

- **Open-ended Questions**

  As you come to an open-ended question, use the Notes pages at the back of the book to do your work. Then fill in the answer using the digits 0-9 and/or the symbols for a decimal point, fraction bar, or negative sign in the answer box provided for each specific open-ended question.

Reference Pages

You may refer to the two preceding Reference Pages as often as you like.

Timing

For the actual test you will be given two 80-minute periods to complete the test, with a ten-minute break in between. However, anyone who has not finished will be allowed to continue working.

Checking Your Answers

You will find the correct answers, along with detailed explanations, for this practice test on page 260.

Reviewing Your Work

When finished, turn to the grid on page 306. Circle the number of any questions that you missed in Test B. You will be able to see a pattern that shows which Benchmarks will need your further attention.

1 Solve for x.

$$5(2x-1)-3=2(4x+1)$$

2 The equation for the height of a toy spacecraft launched vertically into the air is

$h = -16t^2 + 64t$.

The height is measured in feet, while the time is measured in minutes. How long does it take for the spacecraft to reach a height of 64 feet above the ground?

F. 2 minutes

G. 3 minutes

H. 5 minutes

I. 10 minutes

3 Which of the following is the solution to

$4x^2 - 9 = 0$?

A. $\left\{-\dfrac{1}{2}, \dfrac{3}{2}\right\}$

B. $\left\{\dfrac{1}{2}, -\dfrac{3}{2}\right\}$

C. $\left\{-\dfrac{3}{2}, \dfrac{3}{2}\right\}$

D. $\left\{-\dfrac{3}{2}, 2\right\}$

Go On

4 Simplify: $\left(4x^2 - 8x + 9\right) - \left(x^2 + 11x - 6\right)$.

F. $3x^2 - 19x + 15$

G. $4x^2 - x + 6$

H. $5x^2 - x + 12$

I. $5x^2 - x - 12$

5 Express the ratio 15 to 27 as a fraction in simplest form.

A. $\dfrac{5}{9}$

B. $\dfrac{3}{2}$

C. $\dfrac{14}{21}$

D. $\dfrac{21}{14}$

6 A line contains the points $(-4, 8)$ and $(-3, 6)$. What is the x value of the point with a y-value of -10?

Go On ▶

7 Set R = {a, b, c, f, g, k} and

Set V = {d, e, k}.

Which set represents the intersection of these two sets?

A. {a, b, c, d, f, g, h, k}

B. {a, b, d, h, l}

C. {a, v}

D. {k}

8 What is the supplement of a 40° angle?

F. 50°

G. 40°

H. 140°

I. 320°

9 Solve for x.

$$2(3x-1)-(2x+1)<9$$

A. $x<3$

B. $x<-3$

C. $x>-3$

D. $x>3$

10 What is the value of y, given the following?

$y = 3x - 5$

$4x + 2y = -40$

F. -20

G. -14

H. -3

I. 5

11 What is the vertex of the graph of

$y = 4x^2 + 12x - 1?$

A. $\left(-\dfrac{3}{2}, -10\right)$

B. $\left(\dfrac{3}{2}, -10\right)$

C. $(7, 1)$

D. $(-1, -19)$

12 Simplify.

$(4x - y + 8) - (2y - 3) - 2x + 1$

F. $2x - 3y + 12$

G. $x - 2y - 17$

H. $4x - 7y + 5$

I. $4x - 3y - 15$

13 What is the simplified ratio of 2 yards to 10 inches, given 36 inches is equivalent to 1 yard? Express your answer as a decimal.

14 Simplify.

$\sqrt[4]{320,000}$

F. $12\sqrt[4]{2}$

G. $20\sqrt{2}$

H. $100\sqrt[3]{4}$

I. $20\sqrt[4]{2}$

15 Which of the following is false, based upon this Venn diagram?

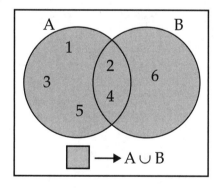

A. $A \cup B = \{1, 2, 3, 4, 5, 6\}$

B. $A = \{1, 2, 3, 4, 5\}$

C. $B = \{2, 4, 6\}$

D. $A \cap B = \{2, 4, 6\}$

Go On ▶

16   What is the midpoint of the segment connecting $(-5,8)$ and $(5,-2)$?

   F. $(2,4)$

   G. $(-1,4)$

   H. $(0,3)$

   I. $(-8,6)$

17   Solve for P.

   $A = P + \mathrm{Pr}t$

   A. $AP-\mathrm{Pr}$

   B. $A+P-\mathrm{Pr}$

   C. $\dfrac{A}{1+rt}$

   D. $\mathrm{Pr}(A-P)$

18   What is the slope of the following line? $5x - 2y = 10$

   Express your answer as a decimal.

19   What is the slope of a line perpendicular to the line? $5x - 2y = 10$

   Express your answer as a decimal.

20 Which of the following graphs represents the line

$3x - 2y = 6$?

F.

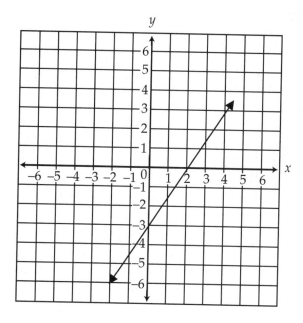

G.

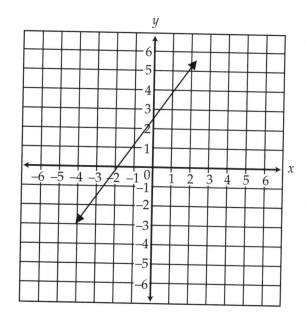

Go On

H.

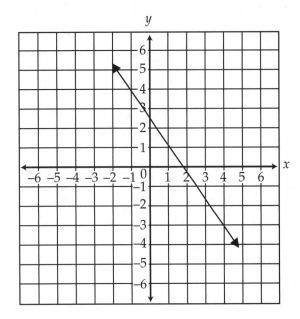

I.

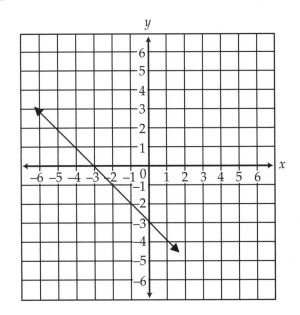

21 Solve the proportion for x.

$$\frac{20}{21} = \frac{x}{3x - 6}$$

  A. $x = -\dfrac{5}{6}$

  B. $x = -5$

  C. $x = \dfrac{40}{13}$

  D. $x = 20$

22 Simplify.

$$14\sqrt{7} - 3\sqrt{3} - 2\sqrt{7} + \sqrt{3}$$

  F. $12\sqrt{7} - 2\sqrt{3}$

  G. $4\sqrt{7} + 4\sqrt{3}$

  H. 30

  I. $7\sqrt{11} - 3$

Go On

23   Which set is the complement of B?

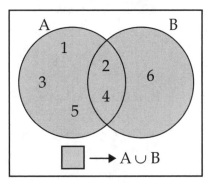

A.   {1, 3, 5}

B.   {2, 4}

C.   {1, 2, 3, 4, 5}

D.   {6}

24   What is the diagonal, in feet, of a square with each side measuring $6\sqrt{2}$ feet?

25   Solve for x.

$$\frac{1}{2}(6x - 4) = \frac{2}{5}x + \frac{1}{3}$$

A. $x = -\dfrac{6}{7}$

B. $x = -\dfrac{7}{6}$

C. $x = -1$

D. $x = \dfrac{35}{39}$

26 Given $f(x) = -\dfrac{3}{5}x + 9$, what is $f(10)$?

```
┌──┬──┬──┬──┬──┬──┬──┐
│  │  │  │  │  │  │  │
└──┴──┴──┴──┴──┴──┴──┘
```

27 Della went to the store to buy 3 pens and 6 notebooks. She spent $20.25. Felipe went to the same store and bought 4 pens and 5 notebooks. He spent $18.75. How much did 1 pen cost?

A. $.75

B. $1.25

C. $2.75

D. $4.00

28 $\dfrac{12x^2 - 16x}{4x} =$

F. $9x + 4$

G. $9x - 12$

H. $3x - 4$

I. $3x + 4$

Go On ▶

29 Simplify.

$$\frac{25x^3yz^4 - 35xy^2z^5 + 40xy^3z^{10}}{5xyz^2}$$

A. $20x^2z^2 - 30yz^3 + 35y^2z^8$

B. $5x^2z^2 - 30yz^3 + 35y^2z^8$

C. $5x^2z^2 - 7yz^3 - 7y^2z^8$

D. $5x^2z^2 - 7yz^3 + 8y^2z^8$

30 Simplify $7\sqrt{6} - \sqrt{3}\left(-2\sqrt{3}\right) - 7\sqrt{2}\left(\sqrt{3}\right)$.

31 Set A = {1, 5, 10} and Set B = {a, e}.

What is A × B?

A. {1, 5, 8, 10, a, e}

B. {(1, a), (1, e), (5, a), (5, e), (8, a), (8, e), (10, a), (10, e)}

C. { }

D. {(1, a), (5, a), (10, a), (1, e), (5, e), (10, e)}

32 What is the x-intercept of the following?

$5x - 2y = 10$

33 Which of the following represents the quantity 4 times the difference between 8 and an unknown?

A. $4(8 + x)$

B. $4x - 8$

C. $4 - 8x$

D. $4(8 - x)$

34 Given $f(x) = -3x + 10$, what is $f(-2)$?

35 What is the complete factorization of $12x^2 - x - 1$?

A. $(3x-1)(4x+1)$

B. $(3x+1)(4x+1)$

C. $(3x-1)(4x-1)$

D. $(3x+1)(4x-1)$

Go On ▶

36 $(3x-8)(3x+8) =$

   F. $9x^2 - 64$

   G. $9x^2 + 64$

   H. $9x^2 - 48x - 64$

   I. $9x^2 - 48x + 64$

37 Della has 10 pencils for every 8 books she has. If Della has 12 books, how many pencils does she have?

38 Simplify $\sqrt[3]{16x^9 y^{15} z^{17}}$.

   F. $2x^3 y^9 z^{13}$

   G. $2x^3 y^5 z^5 \sqrt[3]{2z^2}$

   H. $5x^3 y^9 z^{13}$

   I. $5x^2 y^4 z^5 \sqrt[3]{z}$

39 Given $A = \{4, 7, 9, 11\}$ and $B = \{6, 7, 10, 11\}$, what is $A \cap B$?

   A. $\{4, 6\}$

   B. $\{7, 11\}$

   C. $\{4, 6, 9, 10\}$

   D. $\{4, 6, 7, 9, 10, 11\}$

40 How many centimeters are in the perimeter of a hexagon with each side measuring 7 centimeters?

41 What is the y-intercept of the following?

$5x - 2y = 10$

42 What is the range of this circle?

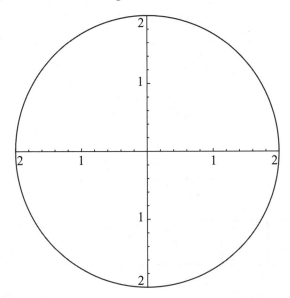

F. all x-values from -2 to 2, including -2 and 2

G. all x-values less than -2 and all x-values greater than 2

H. all y-values between -1 and 1, excluding -1 and 1

I. all y-values from -2 to 2, including -2 and 2

Go On ▶

43 What is the GCF of $14\,x^3 + 42\,x^2$

    A. $7x$

    B. $14x^2$

    C. $144x^3$

    D. x

44 What is the equation of the line that passes through the point $(2, -5)$ and that is perpendicular to the line $3x - 4y = 12$?

    F. $y = \dfrac{-4}{3}x - \dfrac{7}{3}$

    G. $y = \dfrac{-3}{4}x - \dfrac{3}{2}$

    H. $y = \dfrac{3}{4}x + \dfrac{3}{2}$

    I. $y = \dfrac{4}{3}x - \dfrac{7}{3}$

45 What is the simplified ratio of 3 weeks to 6 days, given 7 days equal 1 week? Express your answer as a decimal.

46 Simplify: $\left(x^{-3}y^{4}z^{-1}\right)^{-2}$.

   F. $x^{-5}y^{2}z^{-3}$

   G. $x^{6}y^{2}z^{-2}$

   H. $x^{6}y^{-8}z^{2}$

   I. $x^{9}y^{-16}z$

47 Given U = {1, 3, 5, 7, 9} and B = {3, 5, 7, 9}, what is the complement of B?

   A. {1, 3, 5, 7, 9}

   B. {1, 3}

   C. {1, 3, 9}

   D. {1}

48 If the perimeter of a square is 48 cm, what is its area in square cm?

Go On

49 Below are the graphs of $2x + 3y = -1$

and $4x - y = -9$.

At what point do these two lines intersect?

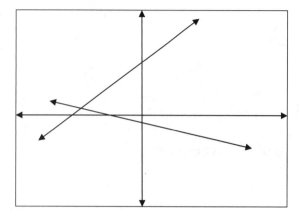

A. $(-2, -1)$

B. $(-2, 1)$

C. $(2, -1)$

D. $(2, 1)$

50 Denver and Moses live 90 miles apart. If they leave their homes at 10:00 AM and drive toward each other, how many miles apart will they be at noon, if Denver drives at 10 miles per hour and Moses drives at 30 miles per hour?

51 The results of Miam's tennis games follow: 7 wins, 3 losses, 5 ties. What is the ratio of her wins to her ties? Express your answer as a decimal.

This is the end of the Mathematics Test.
Until time is called, go back and check your work or answer questions you did not complete. When you have finished, close your Test Book and Answer Book.

Algebra Practice Test Form B

Answer Sheet

1. ☐☐☐☐☐☐☐

2. Ⓕ Ⓖ Ⓗ Ⓘ

3. Ⓐ Ⓑ Ⓒ Ⓓ

4. Ⓕ Ⓖ Ⓗ Ⓘ

5. Ⓐ Ⓑ Ⓒ Ⓓ

6. ☐☐☐☐☐☐☐

7. Ⓐ Ⓑ Ⓒ Ⓓ

8. Ⓕ Ⓖ Ⓗ Ⓘ

9. Ⓐ Ⓑ Ⓒ Ⓓ

10. Ⓕ Ⓖ Ⓗ Ⓘ

11. Ⓐ Ⓑ Ⓒ Ⓓ

12. Ⓕ Ⓖ Ⓗ Ⓘ

13. ☐☐☐☐☐☐☐

14. Ⓕ Ⓖ Ⓗ Ⓘ

15. Ⓐ Ⓑ Ⓒ Ⓓ

16. Ⓕ Ⓖ Ⓗ Ⓘ

17. Ⓐ Ⓑ Ⓒ Ⓓ

18. ☐☐☐☐☐☐☐

19. ☐☐☐☐☐☐☐

20. Ⓕ Ⓖ Ⓗ Ⓘ

21. Ⓐ Ⓑ Ⓒ Ⓓ

22. Ⓕ Ⓖ Ⓗ Ⓘ

23. Ⓐ Ⓑ Ⓒ Ⓓ

24. ☐☐☐☐☐☐☐

25. Ⓐ Ⓑ Ⓒ Ⓓ

26. ☐☐☐☐☐☐☐

27. Ⓐ Ⓑ Ⓒ Ⓓ

28. Ⓕ Ⓖ Ⓗ Ⓘ

29. Ⓐ Ⓑ Ⓒ Ⓓ

30. ☐☐☐☐☐☐☐

31. Ⓐ Ⓑ Ⓒ Ⓓ

32. ☐☐☐☐☐☐☐

33. Ⓐ Ⓑ Ⓒ Ⓓ

34. ☐☐☐☐☐☐☐

35. Ⓐ Ⓑ Ⓒ Ⓓ

36. Ⓕ Ⓖ Ⓗ Ⓘ

37. ☐☐☐☐☐☐☐

38. Ⓕ Ⓖ Ⓗ Ⓘ

39. Ⓐ Ⓑ Ⓒ Ⓓ

40. ☐☐☐☐☐☐☐

41. ☐☐☐☐☐☐☐

42. Ⓕ Ⓖ Ⓗ Ⓘ

43. Ⓐ Ⓑ Ⓒ Ⓓ

44. Ⓕ Ⓖ Ⓗ Ⓘ

45. ☐☐☐☐☐☐☐

46. Ⓕ Ⓖ Ⓗ Ⓘ

47. Ⓐ Ⓑ Ⓒ Ⓓ

48. ☐☐☐☐☐☐☐

49. Ⓐ Ⓑ Ⓒ Ⓓ

50. ☐☐☐☐☐☐☐

51. ☐☐☐☐☐☐☐

Go On ▶

Answers
Practice Test

Practice Test Form B: Answers and Explanations

---

1   **The answer is 5.**

$5(2x-1)-3=2(4x+1)$

$10x-5-3=8x+2$

$10x-8=8x+2$

$2x=10$

$x=5$

2   **The answer is F.**

$h=-16t^2+64t=64$

$0=16t^2-64t+64$

$0=t^2-4t+4$

$0=(t-2)(t-2)$

$2=t$

3   **The answer is C.**

$4x^2-9=0$

$4x^2=9$

$x^2=\dfrac{9}{4}$

$x=\pm\dfrac{3}{2}$

4   **The answer is F.**

$(4x^2-8x+9)-(x^2+11x-6)=$

$4x^2-8x+9-x^2-11x+6=$

$3x^2-19x+15$

5 **The answer is A.**

$$\frac{15}{27} = \frac{5}{9}$$

6 **The answer is 5.**

The slope of the line containing the 2 points is $\dfrac{6-8}{-3-(-4)} = \dfrac{-2}{-3+4} = \dfrac{-2}{1} = -2$. Using that slope, either point,

and $y = mx + b$, the equation of the line can be determined. Using the slope and the first point, $y = mx + b$.

becomes $8 = -2(-4) + b$. This becomes $8 = 8 + b$, making $b = 0$. The equation of the line is $y = -2x + 0$ or

$y = -2x$. Plugging -10 in for y, $-10 = -2x$ and $x = 5$.

7 **The answer is D.**

The intersection includes the elements in both sets.

8 **The answer is H.**

The sum of supplementary angles is $180°$.

9 **The answer is A.**

$$2(3x-1)-(2x+1)<9$$
$$6x-2-2x-1<9$$
$$4x-3<9$$
$$4x<12$$
$$x<3$$

Go On

10 **The answer is G.**
Substitute:

$4x + 2(3x - 5) = -40$
$4x + 6x - 10 = -40$
$10x - 10 = -40$
$10x = -30$
$x = -3$
Since $x = -3$,
substitute that into $y = 3x - 5$
to get $y = 3(-3) - 5 = -9 - 5 = -14$.

11 **The answer is A.**
The x-value of the vertex is $-\dfrac{b}{2a} = -\dfrac{12}{2(4)} = -\dfrac{12}{8} = -\dfrac{3}{2}$. Then, to find the y-value of the

vertex, put x back into the original function:

$y = 4x^2 + 12x - 1 = 4(-\dfrac{3}{2})^2 + 12(-\dfrac{3}{2}) - 1 = 4\left(\dfrac{9}{4}\right) - 18 - 1 = 9 - 18 - 1 = -10.$

12 **The answer is F.**
$\left(4x - y + 8\right) - \left(2y - 3\right) - 2x + 1$
$4x - y + 8 - 2y + 3 - 2x + 1$
$2x - 3y + 12$

13 **The answer is $\dfrac{36}{5}$, which is equivalent to 7.2.**

$\dfrac{2 \text{ yards}}{10 \text{ inches}} = \dfrac{2\left(36\right) \text{ inches}}{10 \text{ inches}} = \dfrac{72 \text{ inches}}{s} = \dfrac{\overline{36}}{5} = 7.2$

14 **The answer is I.**
$\sqrt[4]{320,000} = \sqrt[4]{10,000(32)} = 10\sqrt[4]{16(2)} = 10(2)\sqrt[4]{2} = 20\sqrt[4]{2}$

Go On ▶

15 **The answer is D.**

Choice A is true, since the union is all of the elements in the diagram. Choice B is true because set A contains those listed elements. Likewise for choice C and set B. Choice D is false because the intersection contains only elements 2 and 4.

16 **The answer is H.**

You should calculate the average of the x's and of the y's to create the midpoint. Note that you only need to find the average of the x's. Only answer choice H contains 0 for the first coordinate of the point.

17 **The answer is C.**

$$A = P + \Pr t$$

$$A = P\left(1 + rt\right)$$

$$\frac{A}{1 + rt} = P$$

18 **The answer is $\frac{5}{2} = 2.5$.**

Convert the equation into slope-intercept form: $y = mx + b$, where m is the slope and b is the y-intercept.

$$5x - 2y = 10$$

$$-2y = -5x + 10$$

$$y = \frac{5}{2}x - 5$$

19 **The answer is $\frac{-2}{5} = -0.4$.**

From the results of #18, the slope of the line $5x - 2y = 10$ is $\frac{5}{2}$. The slope of a line that is perpendicular to this line must be the negative reciprocal of $\frac{5}{2}$, which is $\frac{-2}{5} = -0.4$.

Go On ▶

20 **The answer is F.**
Put the equation in slope-intercept form first.

$3x - 2y = 6$

$-2y = -3x + 6$

$y = -\dfrac{3x}{-2} + \dfrac{6}{-2}$

$y = \dfrac{3}{2}x - 3$

The slope is $\dfrac{3}{2}$, while the y-intercept is -3. A positive slope indicates that the line rises from left to right. Also, note that the y-intercept is negative.

21 **The answer is C.**

$\dfrac{20}{21} = \dfrac{x}{3x - 6}$

$21x = 20(3x - 6)$

$21x = 60x - 120$

$-39x = -120$

$x = -\dfrac{120}{-39} = \dfrac{120}{39} = \dfrac{40}{13}$

22 **The answer is F.**
Combine terms with like radicals:

$14\sqrt{7} - 3\sqrt{3} - 2\sqrt{7} + \sqrt{3}$

$12\sqrt{7} - 2\sqrt{3}$

23 **The answer is A.**
The complement is the elements in the universe not in the given set.

24 **The answer is 12.**
The diagonal of this square splits the square into 2 isosceles right triangles, each with legs measuring $6\sqrt{2}$ feet. The diagonal of the square is the hypotenuse of each isosceles right triangle. The hypotenuse of an isosceles right triangle is always $\sqrt{2}$ times the length of a

congruent leg. Hence, this diagonal will measure $6\sqrt{2}\left(\sqrt{2}\right)=6\sqrt{4}=6\left(2\right)=12$. So, this square has a diagonal of 12 feet.

25 **The answer is D.**

$$\frac{1}{2}\left(6x-4\right)=\frac{2}{5}x+\frac{1}{3}$$

$$3x-2=\frac{2}{5}x+\frac{1}{3}$$

Multiply every term by 15 in order to get rid of the denominators.

$$45x-30=6x+5$$

$$39x=35$$

$$x=\frac{35}{39}$$

26 **The answer is 3.**

$$f\left(10\right)=-\frac{3}{5}\left(10\right)+9=-6+9=3$$

27 **The answer is B.**

$$3p+6n=2025$$

$$4p+5n=1875$$

Working this out in cents saves you from using decimals. Divide the first equation by 3.

$p+2n=675$

Solve the first equation for p, so that a substitution can be made.

$$p=-2n+675$$

$$4p+5n=1875$$

$$4\left(-2n+675\right)+5n=1875$$

$$-8n+2700+5n$$

$$n=1875$$

$$-3n=-825$$

The cost for 1 pen is $p=-2n+675=-2\left(275\right)+675=-550+675=125$. This is in cents; so, the dollar cost of 1 pen is \$1.25.

Go On ▶

28 **The answer is H.**

$$\frac{12x^2 - 16x}{4x} = \frac{12x^2}{4x} - \frac{16x}{4x} = 3x - 4$$

29 **The answer is D.**

$$\frac{25x^3yz^4 - 35xy^2z^5 + 40xy^3z^{10}}{5xyz^2} = \frac{25x^3yz^4}{5xyz^2} - \frac{35xy^2z^5}{5xyz^2} + \frac{40xy^3z^{10}}{5xyz^2} = 5x^2z^2 - 7yz^3 + 8y^2z^8$$

30 **The answer is 6.**

$$7\sqrt{6} - \sqrt{3}\left(-2\sqrt{3}\right) - 7\sqrt{2}\left(\sqrt{3}\right) = 7\sqrt{6} + 2\sqrt{9} - 7\sqrt{6} = 2\sqrt{9} = 2(3) = 6$$

31 **The answer is D.**

A × B requires every element of A matched with every element in B. These points make the set A × B.

Since 3 × 2 = 6, there should be 6 points in A × B. The 3 and 2 are the number of elements in A and B, respectively.

32 **The answer is 2.**

The x-intercept is found by setting y equal to 0.

$5x - 2(0) = 10$

$5x = 10$

$x = 2$

33 **The answer is D.**

This is 4 times a quantity represented by a subtraction.

34 **The answer is 16.**

$$f(-2) = -3(-2) + 10 = 6 + 10 = 16$$

35 **The answer is A.**

If necessary, try each answer until you find the one that multiplies out to the given quantity. Be very careful with the signs.

Go On ▶

36 **The answer is F.**
FOIL: firsts, outers, inners, lasts
The middle terms cancel each other out on this product.

37 **The answer is 15.**
$$\frac{10 \text{ pencils}}{8 \text{ books}} = \frac{x \text{ pencils}}{12 \text{ books}}$$
$$8x = 10(12)$$
$$8x = 120$$
$$x = \frac{120}{8} = 15$$

38 **The answer is G.**
$$\sqrt[3]{16x^9 y^{15} z^{17}} = \sqrt[3]{8(2)x^9 y^{15} z^{15} z^2} = 2x^3 y^5 z^5 \sqrt[3]{2z^2}$$

39 **The answer is B.**
The intersection is the set of all elements that appear in both sets.

40 **The answer is 42.**
A hexagon has 6 sides. The perimeter of a polygon is found by summing the measures of all of the sides. Hence, the perimeter is 6(7 centimeters) = 42 centimeters.

41 **The answer is −5.**
Convert the equation into slope-intercept form: $y = mx + b$, where m is the slope and b is the y-intercept.
$$5x - 2y = 10$$
$$-2y = -5x + 10$$
$$y = \frac{5}{2}x - 5$$

42 **The answer is I.**
The range is all of the y-values.

Go On ▶

43 **The answer is B.**

The GCF, the greatest common factor, is the largest value that divides into each term without a remainder. Be careful. Be sure to get the greatest.

44 **The answer is F.**

Put the equation in slope-intercept form first.

$3x - 4y = 12$

$-4y = -3x + 12$

$y = \dfrac{3}{4}x - 3$

The slope of this line is $\dfrac{3}{4}$. Perpendicular lines have negative reciprocal slopes. A perpendicular line, then, would have a slope of $-\dfrac{4}{3}$. The only choice that works is F.

45 **The answer is $\dfrac{7}{2}$ = 3.5.**

$$\frac{3 \text{ weeks}}{6 \text{ days}} = \frac{3(7)}{6} = \frac{21}{6} = \frac{7}{2} = 3.5$$

46 **The answer is H.**

$$\left(x^{-3} y^4 z^{-1}\right)^{-2} = \left(x^{-3}\right)^{-2} \left(y^4\right)^{-2} \left(z^{-1}\right)^{-2} = x^6 y^{-8} z^2$$

Multiply exponents when a base is raised to a power, then to another power.

47 **The answer is D.**

The complement is the elements in the universe not in the given set.

48 **The answer is 144.**

The perimeter is the sum of the lengths of the sides. Thus, each side is 12 cm. The area of a square is found by squaring the length of the side. Then (12)(12) = 144.

49 **The answer is B.**

Look at the graph. The *x*-value must be negative, while the *y*-value must be positive. Choice B is the only such choice. Both equations are true, with *x* as -2 and *y* as 1.

50 **The answer is 10.**

In the 2 hours from 10:00 AM until noon, Denver will have driven 20 miles and Moses will have driven 60 miles. Since that totals 80 miles, Denver and Moses are still 10 miles apart.

51 **The answer is** $\dfrac{7}{5} = 1.4.$

$$\frac{\text{wins}}{\text{ties}} = \frac{7}{5}$$

Go On

Circle **those** specific numbers for **those** questions you answered incorrectly. Use this chart to determine which areas need **additional work**. You will find an in-depth description of these benchmarks in the Introduction to this book.

Benchmark Classification	Benchmark Assessed in Problems Test A	Benchmark Assessed in Problems Test B
MA.912.A.1.8	1, 2, 42, 43, 44	1
MA.912.A.2.3	1, 2	26, 34
MA.912.A.2.4	3, 4, 5	42
MA.912.A.2.13	1, 2, 4	50
MA.912.A.3.1	6, 7	1, 25
MA.912.A.3.2	6, 7	1
MA.912.A.3.3	8	17
MA.912.A.3.4	9, 10	9
MA.912.A.3.5	11, 12	33
MA.912.A.3.7	16, 17, 18	18
MA.912.A.3.8	13	20
MA.912.A.3.9	14, 15	19, 41
MA.912.A.3.10	16, 17, 18	44
MA.912.A.3.11	19, 20	6
MA.912.A.3.12	13, 14. 15, 16, 17, 18	32
MA.912.A.3.13	20, 21, 22, 51	49
MA.912.A.3.14	21, 22	10
MA.912.A.3.15	21, 22	27
MA.912.A.4.1	23, 24, 25	46
MA.912.A.4.2	26, 27, 28	4, 12, 36
MA.912.A.4.3	29, 30, 31	35, 43
MA.912.A.4.4	32	28, 29
MA.912.A.5.1	31	5, 13, 45, 51
MA.912.A.5.4	33, 34, 35	21, 37
MA.912.A.6.1	36, 37, 38, 39	14, 30, 38
MA.912.A.6.2	36, 37, 38, 39	22
MA.912.A.7.1	40	11
MA.912.A.7.2	41, 42, 43 44	3
MA.912.A.7.8	44	2
MA.912.A.10.1	Assessed throughout	8, 16, 24, 40, 48
MA.912.A.10.2	Assessed throughout	Assessed throughout
MA.912.D.7.1	45, 46, 47, 48	7, 31, 39, 47
MA.912.D.7.2	49, 50	15, 23

25 Test-Taking Strategies

Think of these test-taking strategies as the tools for good test preparation on the Algebra End-of-Course Assessment. As a good test-taker, you need to come up with ways to use this tools to achieve success. You need to strategize! As you read the test, including the instructions, be sure to pay attention to each word.

The exam includes two types of questions: **multiple-choice** and **fill-in response**. You should plan on taking about one minute for each multiple-choice question and a bit more for each fill-in question. Also, remember that while a calculator is provided, you won't want to use it all the time.

Of course, you will always be looking for the best answer on the multiple-choice questions; so, you will need to check each possible answer choice. Be cautious on the fill-in questions. Be sure to answer the question asked!

1. Read each question carefully and be sure to read each answer choice. This way, you will know what form your answer needs to be in. For instance, should it be exact or approximate?

2. Work through each exercise, writing out each step. Then, check all answer choices to select the best one.

3. Eliminate answers that are clearly wrong.

   Example: What is the next number in the sequence $-3, 2, 7, 12, \ldots$?

   A. -15

   B. 0

   C. 13

   D. 17

   You know that the answer must be positive. This way, you can eliminate any negative choices and 0. That eliminates A and B. Then, knowing that each term is 5 more than the previous term, you pick the correct answer: 17: D.

4. As mentioned earlier, check the form of the answer before doing the work, so that you know whether you are looking for an exact answer or an approximate one.

   Example: What is the exact area of a circle with a diameter of 8 cm?

   A. 8 pi sq cm

   B. 16 pi sq cm

   C. 50.24 sq cm

   D. 64 sq cm

   The correct answer is B. The area of a circle is pi times the radius squared. The radius of this circle is 4 cm, one-half the diameter. The question asks for an exact answer; so, the answer is left in pi form.

5. Let's build on that last question. How about this question?

Example: What is the exact area of a circle with a diameter of 8 cm?

A. 16 pi cm

B. 16 pi sq cm

C. 64 cm

D. 64 pi cm

The only possible answer is B, since area is measured in square units.

6. You can always substitute each answer choice back into the equation to determine which answer works.

Example: Solve $4(3x - 1) - 2 = x + 5$.

A. -1

B. 0

C. 1

D. 2

Substituting 1 back in for x renders $4(3(1)-1)-2=1+5$. This leads to $4(3-1) -2 =1+5$, then to $4(2) -2=1+5$, which becomes $6=6$. Hence, choice C is the winner!

7. When solving an equation for a variable, be sure to isolate all terms with that variable on 1 side of the equation, as can be seen below.

Example: Solve for $t: A = P + \text{Pr}t$.

A. $AP - \text{Pr}$

B. $A + P - \text{Pr}$

C. $\dfrac{A-P}{\text{Pr}}$

D. $\text{Pr}(A - P)$

$$A = P + \mathrm{Pr}t$$
$$A - P = \mathrm{Pr}t$$

Then, isolate the variable by any required methods. In this case, division by P and r is required. The result is

$$A - P = \mathrm{Pr}\, t$$
$$\frac{A - P}{\mathrm{Pr}} = t \quad \cdot$$

8. Know standard forms, such as $y = mx + b$. This way, you can easily extract the slope and the y-intercept of any line.

9. When solving inequalities, be sure to flip the inequality symbol whenever you multiply or divide both sides of the inequality by a negative number.

Example:

Solve $7(x + 5) - (x - 4) \le 7x - 3$

A. $x \le 42$

B. $x \le -42$

C. $x \ge -42$

D. $x \ge 42$

$$7(x+5)-(x-4) \le 7x-3$$
$$7x+35-x+4 \le 7x-3$$
$$6x+39 \le 7x-3$$

Next, subtract $7x$ from each side of the inequality to get $-x + 39 \le -3$. Then, subtract 39 from each side to get $-x \le -42$. Finally, divide both sides of this inequality by -1 to get $x \ge 42$, making the correct answer choice D.

10. Know mathematics vocabulary.

Example:

Which of the following could not be a point on the graph of a function with points $(-4,2),(2,-3),(6,-1)$, and $(8,-4)$?

A. $(-4, 1)$

B. $(0,7)$

C. $(-6,-3)$

D. $(-2,-1)$

You must know that a function can have only one y-value for any given x-value. Hence, the correct answer is A, since a point already exists with an x-value of -4.

11. When writing an expression, pay close attention to each word and to the order of the expression. This is especially true with expressions involving subtraction and division. The following example illustrates the importance of reading carefully.

Example:

Juan will have to pay for gas and lodging for his trip. Gas costs \$3.25 per gallon, while the room in the hotel costs \$175 per night. What is the expression that represents the total amount he will pay for gas and lodging, given that he will use g gallons and stay for n nights?

A. $3.25n + 175g$

B. $3.25n - 175g$

C. $3.25g - 175n$

D. $3.25g + 175n$

The correct answer to this is D.

12. Be able to interpret graphs.

Example: What is the domain of this circle?

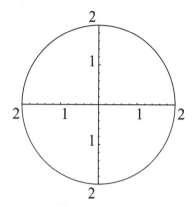

A. All *x*-values from −2 to 2, including −2 and 2

B. All *x*-values less than −2 and all values greater than 2

C. All *y*-values between −1 and 1, excluding −1 and 1

D. All *y*-values less than −2 and all values greater than 2

The domain, the *x*-values, include all values, inclusive, from −2 to 2. Hence, the correct answer is A. This question also requires a command of the vocabulary of mathematics.

13. Solutions to equations are also called answers, roots, and *x*-intercepts.

14. Remember the order of operations. You may have learned the memory device *Please excuse my dear Aunt Sally*. This helpful sentence should mean the following to you:

P: stands for parentheses, brackets, any grouping symbol: Do what is inside these first!

E: stands for exponents and roots: Do any of these next.

MD: stands for multiplication and division, in order, from left to write in this third step.

AS: stands for addition and subtraction, in order, from left to write in this final step.

If the expression you are trying to simplify has a top and bottom, do these separately before writing the simplified form.

Example:

$$\frac{-3^2 - 5(3-4) + \sqrt{9^2 - 3^3 - 5}}{2 - (3^2 - 4)} =$$

$$\frac{-3^2 - 5(-1) + \sqrt{81 - 27 - 5}}{2 - (9-4)} = \frac{-3^2 - 5(-1) + \sqrt{49}}{2 - (5)} = \frac{-9 - 5(-1) + 7}{2 - 5}$$

$$= \frac{-9 + 5 + 7}{2 - 5} = \frac{3}{-3} = -1$$

15. Example: $(4x - 3)^2 =$

A. $8x^2 - 24x - 9$

B. $8x^2 + 24x + 9$

C. $16x^2 - 24x - 9$

D. $16x^2 - 24x + 9$

Write out the steps when working out exercises. This is safer than doing all of the work in your head. On the exercise above, be sure to write out $(4x - 3)(4x - 3)$. Then, FOIL: $16x^2 - 12x - 12x + 9$. Finally, combine like terms to get $16x^2 - 24x + 9$. The correct answer is D.

16. Remember that a fraction is a special ratio. A fraction is the relationship between a part and the whole.

Example: What is the fraction of girls in the set of 12 girls and 18 boys?

A. $\dfrac{2}{5}$

B. $\dfrac{2}{3}$

C. $\dfrac{3}{2}$

D. $\dfrac{5}{2}$

This fraction begins as $\dfrac{12}{30}$. There are 12 girls out of the total number of people: 30. However, once reduced, by dividing the top and bottom each by 6, the result is $\dfrac{2}{5}$. Be sure to reduce all fractions! The correct answer is A.

17. Ratios may be written as follows: 6 to 7 or $\dfrac{6}{7}$ or 6:7.

18. When working on a proportion, 2 equal ratios, be sure to have like-labeled values in corresponding positions on each ratio.

Example:

Mack edits 21 pages in 35 minutes. How many pages should he be able to edit in 20 minutes?

A. 6

B. 10

C. 12

D. 33.3

Each ratio will have pages over minutes. So, $\dfrac{\text{pages}}{\text{minutes}} = \dfrac{21}{35} = \dfrac{p}{20}$. Then, the products of the values on each diagonal must be equal: $35p = 21(20)$, which becomes $35p = 420$. Now, solve the equation by dividing each side by 35 to get $p = 12$. The correct answer is C.

19. Simplify all radicals as much as possible. If necessary, do so in steps.

Example:

Simplify $\sqrt[3]{32{,}000}$.

A. 1,100

B. $20\sqrt[3]{4}$

C. $100\sqrt[3]{4}$

D. $10\sqrt[3]{32}$

$$\sqrt[3]{32,000} = \sqrt[3]{32 \cdot 1,000} = \sqrt[3]{32} \cdot \sqrt[3]{1,000} = \sqrt[3]{32} \cdot 10 = \sqrt[3]{8 \cdot 4} \cdot 10$$
$$= \sqrt[3]{8} \cdot \sqrt[3]{4} \cdot 10 = 2 \cdot \sqrt[3]{4} \cdot 10 = 2 \cdot 10 \cdot \sqrt[3]{4} = 20\sqrt[3]{4}.$$

The correct answer is B. Remember to write out the steps, rather than doing too much in your head!

20. Remember to use the process of elimination.

Example:

Set R = {a, b, c, f, g, k} and Set V = {a, d, f, h}. What set represents the intersection of these two sets?

A. {a, b, c, d, f, g, h, k}

B. {a, b, d, h, l}

C. {a, v}

D. {a, f}

The intersection of a set is the elements that appear in both sets. The smaller set is V. So, the intersection will not have more elements than the number in that set: 4. Eliminate choices A and B. The intersection will not have an element that does not appear in that smaller set. Eliminate choice C, since V does not have an element v. Choice D is correct, since a and f are the only elements that appear in both sets.

21. Know the symbols and vocabulary of set notation.

Example 1:

Set A = {1, 5, 8, 10} and Set B = {a, e, u}. What is A × B?

A. {1, 5, 8, 10, a, e, u}

B. {(1, a), (1, e), (1, u), (5, a), (5, e), (5, u), (8, a), (8, e), (8, u), (10, a), (10, e), (10, u)}

C. { }

D. {(1, a), (5, a), (8, a), (10, a)}

The correct answer is B, since A × B requires every element of A matched with every element in B. These points make the set A × B. Since 4 × 3 = 12, there should be 12 points in A × B. The 4 and 3 are the number of elements in A and B, respectively.

Example 2:

Given A = {4, 7, 9, 11} and B = {6, 7, 10, 11}, what is A ∪ B?

A. {4, 6}

B. {7, 11}

C. {4, 6, 9, 10}

D. {4, 6, 7, 9, 10, 11}

Choice D is correct because A ∪ B requires all of the elements in either A or B or both. This is the union of the 2 sets.

Example 3:

Given A = {4, 7, 9, 11} and B = {6, 7, 10, 11}, what is A ∩ B?

A. {4, 6}

B. {7, 11}

C. {4, 6, 9, 10}

D. {4, 6, 7, 9, 10, 11}

The correct answer is B. A ∩ B, the intersection of the 2 sets, requires all of the elements present in both A and B.

Example 4:

Given U = {1, 3, 5, 7, 9} and B = {5, 7}, what is the complement of B?

A. {1, 3, 5, 7, 9}

B. {1, 3}

C. {1, 3, 9}

D. { }

Choice C is the winner. The complement is all of the elements in the universal set but outside the given set, B in this case. The "leftovers" are 1, 3, and 9.

Example 5:

If $2 \in A$ and $9 \in B$, which of the following is true?

A. $(2, 2) \in A \times B$

B. $A = \{2, 9\}$

C. $B = \{2, 15\}$

D. $(2, 9) \in A \times B$

The correct answer is D. $A \times B$ requires every element of A matched with every element in B. These points make the set $A \times B$. So, 2 from A would be the first coordinate in a point in $A \times B$ and 9 would be the second element in a point in $A \times B$. Thus, the point (2,9) is an element of $A \times B$.

22. Vocabulary is important for the geometry questions, too. You have likely been learning this since before elementary school.

23. Draw pictures on geometry exercises. It helps you to see what is happening.

24. Estimate answers, when possible.

Example: Geometry Standard 1

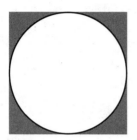

A circle is inscribed in a square. The length of the diameter of the circle is 8 cm. What is the area of the shaded portion of this diagram?

A. (16 − 64 pi) sq cm

B. (64 − 16 pi) sq cm

C. 16 pi sq cm

D. 64 pi sq cm

Using 3 for an approximation for pi, the answer choices are approximately:

A. −176 sq cm

B. 16 sq cm

C. 48 sq cm

D. 192 sq cm

The area of the square is 64 sq cm. The area of the shaded portion is definitely less than that. Eliminate D. Eliminate A, since that is a negative and thus a ridiculous result!

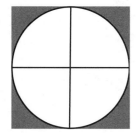

Quartering the diagram, you can see that less than $\frac{1}{2}$ of each quarter is shaded. So, since $\frac{1}{4}$ of 64 is 16, the final answer must be less than 16 sq cm. The only reasonable choice is B.

In fact, choice B shows exactly how the shaded portion is derived: take the area of the square, then subtract the area of the circle.

25. Since you are not penalized for incorrect answers, you should answer every question. Even if you have no idea how to do an exercise, you should guess. You might be lucky!

And here's a final tip: Sit up straight, breathe deeply, and remember that you have learned most, if not all, of what is being asked of you. Give it your best!

NOTES

NOTES